# Yale French Studies

NUMBE

D1548438

# Surrealism and Its Others

# Yale French Studies

Katharine Conley and Pierre Taminiaux, *Special editors for this issue*
Alyson Waters, *Managing editor*
*Editorial board:* Edwin Duval (Chair), Ora Avni, R. Howard Bloch, Thomas Kavanagh, Christopher L. Miller, Donia Mounsef, Jean-Jacques Poucel, J. Ryan Poynter, Julia Prest, Agnieszka Tworek
*Editorial assistant:* Scott J. Hiley
*Editorial office:* 82-90 Wall Street, Room 308
*Mailing address:* P.O. Box 208251, New Haven, Connecticut 06520-8251
*Sales and subscription office:*
Yale University Press, P.O. Box 209040
New Haven, Connecticut 06520-9040
Published twice annually by Yale University Press

Designed by James J. Johnson and set in Trump Medieval Roman by The Composing Room of Michigan, Inc. Printed in the United States of America by the Vail-Ballou Press, Binghamton, N.Y.

ISSN 044-0078
ISBN for this issue 0-300-11072-3

KATHARINE CONLEY AND
PIERRE TAMINIAUX

# Editors' Preface: Surrealism and Its Others

Surrealism was the most prominent avant-garde movement of the twentieth century: its artistic power arguably continues to be felt today in the realms of popular culture, film, photography, poetry, fiction, theater, advertising, politics, postcolonial productions, and theory. Never exclusively a literary or art movement, surrealism was a way of walking down the street, of engaging oneself in politics, of dreaming and living in the everyday. Its most famous arbiter was André Breton, author of surrealism's informal history in the form of the numerous articles he wrote throughout his life (1896–1966), in addition to the two *Manifestoes of Surrealism* he published in 1924 and 1930. Yet it was always a collective movement, both in practice and by ideology, and, as such, there were always those whose work and ideas at times clashed with Breton's mainstream. It was also a movement that remained active, through successive waves of participants, from its inception in the 1920s through the 1960s.

This volume of *Yale French Studies* on "Surrealism and its Others" examines a series of works and theories by writers, artists, and thinkers who positioned themselves and their productions in dialogue with, but also in contradiction to, Breton's surrealism. Martine Antle's essay, "Surrealism and the Orient," looks both at European surrealism's idealization of the Orient and at how Egyptian writers like George Henein and Joyce Mansour respond with their own version of surrealism. Adam Jolles, in "The Tactile Turn," wonders about the contradictions of the surrealists' appreciation for both so-called primitive art and a primitivist aesthetic together with their increasingly committed anti-colonialist stance, which led them away from a visually determined aesthetic and increasingly toward a tactile one. Jonathan Eburne takes up the surrealist's anticolonialism in "Antihumanism and Terror,"

**YFS 109,** *Surrealism and Its Others,* ed. Katharine Conley and Pierre Taminiaux,
© 2006 by Yale University.

first expressed in the 1920s with their support of the anticolonial insurgency of Abd-el-Krim in the Rif section of Morocco and later expressed in essays in support of Algerian independence in the 1950s. Pierre Taminiaux also considers the politics of the surrealists in "Breton and Trotsky," specifically in relation to their use of the word *revolution* as both a political and an aesthetic term. Richard Stamelman studies surrealist aesthetics in "Photography: The Marvelous Precipitate of Desire," in the shape of Brassaï's haunting images of Paris which, despite Brassaï's determined stance as an outsider to the surrealist group, echo ways in which Breton himself expressed desire in his automatic poetry from the earliest phase of the surrealist movement. Surrealist desires as linked to queer expressions of sexuality, both within and outside of the surrealist circle, are more directly analyzed by Robert Harvey in "Where's Duchamp?—Out Queering the Field."

In "From Surrealist Cinema to Surrealism in Cinema," Raphaëlle Moine examines the way in which the term "surrealist" has been linked to a variety of styles of films in recent criticism, and goes back to the origins of surrealist ideas on film and its production. Georgiana Colvile, in "Between Surrealism and Magic Realism," argues for an understanding of André Delvaux's films—only just released on DVD—as surrealist; an outsider to the surrealist group, like Brassaï, Delvaux was clearly in an aesthetic and philosophical dialogue with surrealism's mainstream. Katharine Conley studies the relation between Breton and artists literally labeled outsiders in "Surrealism and Outsider Art," by going back to Breton's early efforts to clarify surrealist automatism in opposition to spiritist automatism, which paradoxically produced work later labeled *art brut* that became absorbed into an increasingly globalized surrealist aesthetic.

A drawing by a spiritist medium, Mme. Fondrillon, graces the cover of this issue because her automatic work exemplifies surrealism's others. Breton and the surrealists sought emphatically to distinguish the automatic drawings produced by members of their group like André Masson from those produced by mediums seeking to communicate with other worlds. At the same time Breton used this very drawing twice—once in the issue of *La révolution surréaliste*, where he announced the existence of surrealist painting and art, and once again in *Minotaure* eight years later, when, paradoxically, he was again distinguishing surrealist from mediumistic automatism. Surrealism always sought to distinguish itself from other movements and ideologies and yet, as Breton's use of Mme. Fondrillon's drawings indicates, its members often celebrated their commonalities with the many "others" outside of the official group with whom they shared passions—from mediums to Marxists, visual artists, filmmakers, and ethnographers.

This collection of essays celebrates those who helped Breton and the surrealists define the movement through their differences during the fifty years in which surrealism was established, and beyond. For surrealist anticolonialist thinking, its appreciation of outsider art, its fascination with non-Western cultures and art, its dream logic in poetry, visual art, photography, and film, its fascination with the marvelous in everyday life *within* reality as well as in opposition to it, continue to mark contemporary culture. Each one of the writers, artists, and thinkers examined here was influenced in his or her surrealism by the collective and open spirit of the movement, as defined by Breton himself in the first *Manifesto* of 1924 and through his essays. They were all at least temporarily associated with surrealism, even if primarily in an oppositional or questioning role. In some cases this outside perspective comes from a European country outside France—from as close as Belgium; in other cases it comes from further away—from North Africa or Latin America, and thus reflects surrealism's engagement with non-European, formerly colonized cultures, reinforcing surrealism's staunchly anticolonialist stance and fundamentally confirming surrealism as more than an aesthetic phenomenon: it was also, and perhaps more importantly, a powerful political and social reality as well. The artists, writers, and theorists examined here were all, in some way, outsiders to surrealism and at the same time close to it. Each one thus delivers a new perspective on this avant-garde, modernist movement. They help to define surrealism's gaze outward while simultaneously serving to sharpen how surrealism as a growing and developing movement looked gazing inward, from the outside.

MARTINE ANTLE

# Surrealism and the Orient

Occident tu es condamné à mourir. Nous sommes les vainqueurs de
l'Europe. Laisse l'Orient, ta terreur, répondre à nos espoirs enfin!
—Louis Aragon

You, West, are condemned to die. We have been victorious in Europe.
Let the Orient, your terror, finally answer our hopes![1]

André Breton's declarations and the numerous political views pro-
nounced by the surrealists during the Rif War[2] (1919–26) in Morocco
marked a turning point in their thinking and awareness of the Orient,
which partially explains the central place that the Orient occupies in
the surrealist imagination. The Orient, like Artaud's Mexico, is a magical realm and is part of the "new myth" proclaimed by Breton and his
group in the text *Rupture inaugurale,* on June 21, 1947. An inquiry in
*Cahiers du mois,* published in 1924, demonstrates this fact. In the
piece, Breton clashes with Henri Massis, who had announced that the
Orient constituted a true menace for the West. Breton, taking a radical,
antinationalist position, proclaims the death of Western rationalism
and literally predicts the "liquidation" of Western Mediterranean influences, notably ancient Greece and Rome: "For my part, I'm pleased
that Western civilization is at stake. Today light comes to us from the
Orient. . . . The *liquidation* of Mediterranean influences is underway
and for that I can only rejoice."[3]

These provocative declarations lay the groundwork for an oriental
myth that will remain nearly invisible throughout the surrealist movement. For Breton, the Orient will henceforth be at odds with the rational West; he proposes an idealized form of Eastern thought as an antidote to the evils of Western civilization. Breton's prophecies echo those

1. All quotations given in both French and English are my own translations.
2. The Rif War is also known as the War of Melilla.
3. André Breton, *Oeuvres complètes* I (Paris: Gallimard, 1988), 898, emphasis mine.

**YFS 109,** *Surrealism and Its Others,* ed. Katharine Conley and Pierre Taminiaux,
© 2006 by Yale University.

of Artaud who contributed to the same myth opposing the rational mind to the culture of the Other. Artaud and Breton, like many other intellectuals between the two World Wars, pondered the question of the Other; they responded to the "call of diversity" which, according to Édouard Glissant, corresponds to the first steps leading to a reflection on alterity in the West.

Presuming that one subscribes to Breton's ideas, the Orient would appear to be a true catalyst of the surrealist movement as well as an essential driving force and source of inspiration. In his "Introduction au discours sur le peu de réalité" (1924), Breton once again stresses this motivation of surrealism, namely the Orient and its symbols, while calling upon his muse: "Orient, victorious Orient, you who have only symbolic value, do with me as you please. Orient of anger and pearls! Orient, lovely bird of prey and of innocence, I implore you from the depths of the kingdom of shadows! inspire me!"[4]

There was an indisputable presence of an Oriental leitmotif in surrealism, of which Breton's *Nadja* would be the prototype: the text repeatedly overlaps with *A Thousand and One Nights* through its recourse to the theme of wandering, the dream, the woman being the initiator, and the fortuitous meeting. In spite of these ostentatious declarations, the Orient remains nonetheless a quasi-ephemeral phenomena of the movement. It is important to note that the attraction of the Oriental myth quickly wanes for the surrealists and, when all is said and done, it serves anticolonialism. Here, a notable discrepancy separates early 1920s official discourse on the Orient and an eventual overture to the Orient which would spark a dialogue or exchange with the Other. Representations of the Orient in surrealism are hinted at in the fringes of the movement, as we shall later see when we examine the work of Unica Zürn, or are recovered from the Orientalist yoke that permeates the period's popular culture.

To shed light on the connections that surrealism maintained with the Orient, one must first examine the potential implications of surrealism in the region. A fundamental question remains: to what degree was surrealism able to establish a fertile ground for poetry and oriental art?

---

4. Breton, *Oeuvres complètes II* (Paris: Gallimard, 1992), 280.

## SURREALIST ENCOUNTERS WITH THE MIDDLE EAST

Unlike with "Negro-African poetry," which was expressly championed by Breton, no pure symbiosis existed between surrealist and Arabic poetry, which remained deeply rooted in classic tradition until the 1950s. It was not until the late 1950s that the Lebanese poet Unsi Al-Hajj broke with the tradition of monorhyme poetry and began experimenting with the prose poem. In the 1960s, he translated Artaud and Breton into Arabic and in doing so, introduced them to the Arab world. Moreover, if vanguard poetic revolutions were absent from Arabic literature during the first generation of surrealism, it was because the movement was not easily integrated into the literary circles of French colonies and protectorates. In his work analyzing the points of convergence between surrealism and North Africa, Hédi Abdel-Jaouad explains, "for the colonized man slaving away under the yoke of colonialism, surrealist manifestations seemed like a bourgeois luxury."[5] Yet, in spite of this distrust of the European avant-garde, francophone North African literature of the post-World-War-II era was able to benefit from surrealism; it made itself permeable to the movement's innovations, symbols, writing process, and it also relied on the surrealist principles of rupture and subversion. Texts such as *La voyeuse interdite* by Nina Bouraoui (1991) borrow their metaphorical and semantic derivations from surrealism. Among the numerous encounters between surrealism and North African francophone writing, we can also count the shared symbolism of the star, specifically in the works of Breton and Kateb Yacine. Bernard Aresu confirms this coming together: "The extent to which Breton and Kateb's imaginative procedure relies on the ontological and generative properties of a shared image is striking."[6]

Among all the countries of the Middle East, Egypt remained the country of predilection for surrealism throughout the vanguard period. Indeed, in Egypt surrealism was spread by writer and painter Georges Henein (1914–1973) who joined the movement in 1936 and then founded the movement Art et liberté in 1937 with three other artists:

5. Hédi Abdel-Jaouad, *Fugues de barbarie. Les écrivains maghrébins et le surréalisme* (New York-Tunis: Les mains secrètes, 1998), 51.
6. Aresu, *Counterhegemonic Discourse from the Maghreb: The Poetics of Kateb's Fiction* (Tübingen: Verlag, 1993), 36.

Ramsès Younane, Fouad Kamel, and Kamel el-Telmessany.[7] These surrealist beginnings in Egypt were aimed first and foremost at the Egyptian francophone community living in Egypt.

The group's first illustrated bulletin came out in March 1939, with bilingual texts in Arabic and French. Like surrealism, Art et liberté had its own manifesto (1938) with photos and group declarations. The Egyptian surrealist movement also considered art to be a principal motivating factor of all revolutions, as we can see in the following collective declaration:

> It is known that the current society looks upon any new artistic and literary creation with loathing as long as it threatens the cultural establishment whether intellectually or conceptually. . . . O men of art, men of letters, let us stand together and accept the challenge. We must stand in the ranks of "bad art" for in it is all the hope for the future.[8]

In 1941, Egypt's independent art movement identifies three principal objectives. First, to renew art in order to "respond in every way possible to the appalling wave of academic painting"; second, loyal to the myth of childhood that the surrealists laid out in the paintings of de Chirico (especially *Mélancolie et mystère d'une rue*), the Egyptian surrealists grant a privileged place to childhood and seek "children's insatiable curiosity"; finally, they extol the internationalism of their movement. From here, it is a matter of

> integrating the activity of Egypt's young artists into the expansive circuit of modern art, passionate and vibrant, which rebels against any police, religious, or commercial instruction, the art whose pulse is felt in New York, London, and Mexico City, in every place where the Diego Rivieras, Paalens, Tanguys, and Henry Moores fight, everywhere that men have yet to despair of the total freedom of the human consciousness.[9]

These intentions to liberate the world through art were modeled on the claims of the European vanguard and have had a more noticeable impact on painting than on literature. Egyptian surrealism would play a fundamental role in the evolution of abstract art in Egypt; it is actu-

7. Their respective works are reproduced in Samir Gharieb's *Surrealism in Egypt and Plastic Arts* (Guizeh, Egypt: Prism Publications, 1986).

8. Samir Gharieb, "Long Live Bad Art," in *Surrealism in Egypt and Plastic Arts*, 77–78.

9. "La désagrégation des mythes," in *Passages, recueil de textes en hommage à Ramsès Younane*, not paginated. (Cairo: Ministère de la Culture, 1998).

ally thanks to the group Art et liberté that modern art and the pursuit of abstraction were introduced in Egypt in the following decades.

With his colleague Ramsès Younane (1913–1966), according to whom surrealism is "the means to create a new mythology reconciling reality and legend,"[10] Georges Henein distributed the magazine *La part du sable.* The two also collaborated with Breton on a leaflet published in 1938 entitled "Pour un art révolutionnaire indépendant." Ramsès Younane and Georges Henein both signed the *Rupture inaugurale* with the surrealists on June 21, 1947.

Part of the second generation of surrealists, Henein no longer found it necessary to experiment with the possibilities of automatic writing. Nonetheless, he places surrealist humor, eroticism, and alchemy at the heart of his poetry. For example, his poem "La femme intérieure"[11] employs electric metaphors that picture shock, a governing idea in surrealist poetry: "Belle comme la foudre, s'arrêtant à mi-ciel" [Beautiful like lightning, stopping in mid-sky].

Henein reads the works of contemporary Egyptians with a European surrealist slant; he links them, as he does poet Joyce Mansour, who was of Egyptian descent, to the movement. Although he remarks certain surrealist accents in Mansour's work, such as "the rigorous cruelty of childhood," and gives her a central position in a fictive society of "Black Humor,"[12] he does not bring out the roots of her multicultural identity which, as Katharine Conley has demonstrated, "proves to be the heart of her poetic specificity."[13]

This surge of surrealism in Egypt is not limited to the francophone Egyptian community. Indeed, Henein presents several conferences on surrealism in Arabic in Cairo and in 1940 starts the Arab-language magazine *Al-Tattawor.* The magazine will have nine issues. What sets the surrealist Egyptian group apart, as Sarane Alexandrian meticulously demonstrates,[14] is that, even though most of the texts are written in French for a francophone audience in Egypt and France, surrealism sub-

10. "L'art indépendant en Egypte," in *Passages, recueil de textes en hommage à Ramsès Younane,* not paginated.

11. Georges Henein, "La femme intérieure," in *La force de saluer* (Paris: Éditions de la différence, 1978), 53.

12. Heinein, "L'esprit frappeur. Carnets 1940–1973 (Paris: Encre Éditions, 1980), 80.

13. Katharine Conley, "La femme-amphore de Joyce Mansour," in *Entre Nil et Sable. Écrivains d'Égypte d'expression française (1920–1960),* (Paris: Centre National de Documentation Pédagogique, 1999), 206.

14. See in particular Sarane Alexandrian, *Georges Henein Collection Poètes d'aujourd'hui* (Paris: Seghers, 1981), 7–85.

sequently developed in the Arabic language.[15] By placing the Arabic language on the same level as French, Henein introduces an unprecedented critical issue—the question of cultural duality and bilingualism. He places the question of belonging and identity at the forefront of his reflections and advises Eastern intellectuals to scour literature on the Orient for elements other than the traditional, often futile, images of their "unexpressed" world. According to Henein, Egyptian surrealism differentiates itself from other movements of Modernity precisely through its linguistic and cultural "betweenness" that writers must address:

> We are experiencing two simultaneous movements, which cannot be considered absolutely contradictory. On the one hand, the Arabic language is resurfacing and affirming itself as a passionate connection and instrument of independence; on the other, the need of modernity gives rise to a dual cultural belonging that forces [these writers] to rely on a foreign language.[16]

Exploration of a dual cultural belonging expands the frontiers of Egyptian surrealism since it places it in direct context with cultural difference, a notion swept under the rug throughout the history of the European movement. For, what do we really know about European surrealists' travels if it is not that they maintain their Eurocentric point of view in discovering other cultures? They hardly considered intercultural questions at the time of their travels and, like "allegorists," as Tzvetan Todorov might say, they remained mostly preoccupied by their own culture. The travel journal Breton kept during his stay with the Hopi Indians serves to illustrate the surrealists' lack of interest in striking up a dialogue with the Other. This journal takes the form of a tourist diary, and from day to day Breton relates his perpetually "external" point of view regarding the Hopis. Likewise, during his stay with the Tarahumara Indians, Artaud records a priest's speech from a ritual ceremony. Although in indirect discourse and French, he insists that the text is "authentic."[17] Max Ernst's 1924 trip to the Far East with Paul Eluard and Gala does not seem to have influenced his pictorial

15. These exchanges take place during a fertile period for cultural exchange between Egypt and Europe. In the feminist press, there is an expansion of bilingual publications, namely L'Égyptienne, féminisme-sociologie-art in the 1920s and The New Woman (La Femme Nouvelle) in the 1940s.

16. Henein, L'esprit frappeur, 142.

17. See my article "Artaud et le primitivisme," in Antonin Artaud. Modernités d'Antonin Artaud (Paris: Minard, 2000), 169–79.

works, with the exception of certain evocative titles of paintings: "Aux 100000 Colombes, "La fleur du désert," and "Une nuit d'amour."

Interestingly, the surrealists were encouraged to rethink the Orient because of the presence of the Algerian artist Baya Mehieddine (1931–) in Paris. Baya, a self-taught artist, was introduced to vanguard artistic milieus in Paris in the 1940s and was immediately noticed by Breton and Picasso, with whom she remained in close contact. Picasso in fact started his series of "Women of Algiers" in 1954 shortly after meeting her. Baya exhibited in Paris in 1947 at the Maeght Gallery, which had opened only two years previously. She was at the center of artistic attention and gained great visibility from her inclusion in the *Dictionary of Surrealism*, in which very few women artists were listed. Baya clearly expressed her intentions to move away from Braque's or Matisse's colors and to explore those of Kabyle women's traditional clothing, such as turquoise blue or Indian pink ("Femme et poisson volants," 1947). In her work, Baya stages her own personal mythology and places women at the center of her canvasses. Her female characters populate the same natural world as birds, fish, and plants ("Femme robe jaune oiseau en main," 1947).[18] The female bodies and the objects she paints form intricate decorative and repetitive rhythmic patterns reminiscent of Arabic calligraphy, Islamic Art, and oriental carpets. These patterns give birth to intertwined floral and foliate figures. The women's faces in her canvasses are indistinguishable from the white background and are delineated only by the shape of the eye, which itself mimics an inverted letter H in Arabic. It is interesting to note that, when learning to write the Arabic letter H, children are told to draw an eye. The letter H also denotes a call for attention in the Arabic language. Baya's representation of the female eye in the shape of an inverted H suggests an alternative mode of seeing and of reading, an alternative to art produced by vanguard male artists and to colonial representations of Oriental women.

Baya's art resists conventional Western categorizations of art in spite of the fact that she has been exoticized and labeled by many Western critics as a "naïve" or "primitive" painter. On the contrary, Baya invites us to read new forms of artistic creation that are grounded in a complex history of traditions characterized by Persian miniatures, Arabic art, and Arabo-Berber cultures of Algeria. Breton's interpretation of Baya's art reveals the ambiguous and sometimes contradictory position

18. Baya's works are reproduced in *Baya* (Paris: Maeght Éditeur, 1998).

that the surrealists took concerning the Orient. While Breton rightly recognizes the Berber origins and "ancient Egyptian traditions" of Baya's pictorial works, he also endows her with certain attributes of the surrealist woman, notably the woman-child, the sorceress, the clairvoyant: "Baya's secret differs not at all from that of Michelet's heroine. . . . She is clairvoyant at times. . . . The lowered eyes on love struck flowers, a young flower herself."[19] Even more revealing is the fact that Breton redefines Baya, in an Orientalist and fantastic *Thousand and One Nights* perspective. Baya, "lifting a corner of the veil," is a pretext used to stir up clichés of "Happy Arabia": "it is undeniable [attests Breton] that her paraphernalia of wonders . . . secretly takes part in extracts of perfumes from the *Thousand and One Nights*" (Baya, 12). In spite of these attempts of recovery for the benefit of the surrealists, Baya remained loyal to her pictorial technique and did not model her work on the principles or techniques of Western painting. An exoticized object in Europe, she overlapped with the surrealist project through her exploration of the realm of dreams. At the same time, she enriched surrealism with her motifs and colors reaching back to folkloric and Arabo-Berber traditions for which the vanguard milieus hardly recognized her. As Sana 'Makhoul demonstrates, it is also possible that Parisian artistic milieus seized on Baya to protest colonization in Algeria and to free themselves from the unease and sense of guilt experienced by intellectuals of the period: "French intellectual circles took a particular interest in Baya's work not only because she is an Algerian woman. Maybe there is some feeling of guilt that is tangled in her case."[20]

## REPRESENTATIONS OF THE ORIENT IN SURREALISM

If it constitutes an ephemeral and quasi-invisible theme in the first two generations of surrealism,[21] the Middle East will eventually assert its

19. Breton, "Baya," in *Baya*, 11–12.

20. Sana 'Makhoul. "Baya Mahieddine: An Arab Woman Artist," *Detail. A Journal of Art Criticism Published by the South Bay Area Women's Caucus for Art* 6/1 (Fall 1998): 4.

21. And not to mention certain imitations of Surrealism such as the work of English painter Philip Bouchard. During his trips to Saudi Arabia in the 1970s and 1980s, he recreated certain landscapes of de Chirico and Dali that he deliberately placed in the Middle East. In particular, "A House in the Desert" (1982), "Chequerboard in Dir'iyah" (1979), and "Houses on the Red Sea" (1981). Philip Bouchard, *From Surrealism to Orientalism. The Influence of Arabia on the Work of an Artist* (London: Immel Publishing, 1985).

presence on the fringes of the founding movement, and the geography of the Orient will also open to the Far East.

Hannah Höch, the Berliner who, favoring Africa and Indonesia, works on the construction and performance of races and gender in her photomontages, devotes nonetheless two photomontages to the Far and Middle East.[22] In the first, entitled "Chinese Girl with a Fan" (1926), she shows the smiling face of a young Chinese girl which is transferred through the movement of several superposed fans. In this way, she invites the spectator to reflect on the question and the play of visibility and invisibility of the Asian figure in the representation of the vanguard.

The second photomontage, entitled "Homage to Riza Abasi" was created later, in 1963. This photomontage presents the face of the actress Audrey Hepburn on the occasion of the release of her movie *Roman Holiday*, as it was printed in the German newspaper *B.Z* on November 10, 1953. While the press of the period had placed Hepburn directly above the bikini-clad body of a popular contemporary model, Höch juxtaposes Hepburn's face with the hypersexualized body of a belly dancer. This photomontage parodies the Orientalist odalisques who also depended upon Western models. In addition, it denounces the continual sexualization of the Orient. The photomontage technique therefore stresses the staging and the construction of the Orient. Furthermore, the title of the photomontage ("Homage to Riza Abasi") directly alludes to the seventeenth century Persian miniaturist Riza-I-Abbasi, pointing out that the Orient and its character representations go back to Arabo-Persian tradition and not to representations driven by Orientalism.

Another Berliner, Unica Zürn, will use the Orient as a model in her novel *The Man of Jasmine, Impressions from a Mental Illness*.[23] In this text, Zürn fulfills Breton's prophecies in making the Orient a decisive factor in artistic creation. With the *Man of Jasmine*, an anti-establishment text that seeks new modes of expression, new identities and geographic markers such as the Far or Middle East upset the ethnocentric references of surrealist culture.

In *The Man of Jasmine*, the Orient is not presented as an exotic

22. Hannah Höch's works are reproduced in *The Photomontages of Hannah Höch*. Volume organized by Maria Makela and Peter Boswell (Minneapolis: Walker Art Center, 1997).
23. Unica Zürn, *The Man of Jasmine, Impressions from a Mental Illness*, trans. Malcolm Green (Channel Islands: Guernsey Press, 1994).

place, but rather as an intercultural space where many races merge: "from Red Indian, Oriental or Asian races." The motif of jasmine, an Asian plant, and other Oriental motifs that emerge from the text take part in a process of disorientation and delocalization. Jasmine, which serves as a unifying thread, guides us throughout the narrator's experience in an asylum. It is important to remember that jasmine is highly prized both in the Orient and in Asia. In Persian and Arab tradition, jasmine is one of the principal plants that evoke amorous passion. Its perfume is "at the crossroads of hygienic products, beauty, and eroticism."[24] In her often fruitless search for childhood memories, the narrator of *Man of Jasmine* repeatedly reconnects with the places of her past to rediscover the furniture of her childhood brought from the Orient and collected by her father:

> She spends the night recollecting her old childhood memories with a wondrous clarity. . . . She walks up and down the stairs, through all twelve rooms, and gazes into the winter fire of the large hall. She touches the Asian and Arabian furniture her father had brought back from his travels. (47)

From that moment on, the Orient sparks thought and leads to the creation of several anagrams with a jasmine motif. Reflection is also directly associated with the jasmine in the text that, like *Nadja*, functions on chance and a fortuitous encounter in Paris: "A few days later she experiences the first miracle in her life: in a room in Paris she finds herself standing before the Man of Jasmine. The shock of this encounter is so great that she is unable to get over it" (27). The Orient and/or jasmine remain the versatile thread that guides the narrator throughout the story. This oriental motif that fed the narrator's childhood imagination occasionally becomes threatening, and can become instead a trap. The childhood dream then becomes a nightmare. Imprisoned and seeking liberty, the narrator tries in vain to open a door: "But she finds it impossible to open the door . . . she makes three deep, ceremonious bows before the door and speaks the old formula from the tale of the *Thousand and One Nights:* 'Open Sesame'! But this door will not open and she keeps repeating her little ceremony until she is exhausted. In vain!" (54).

In *The Man of Jasmine,* the Orient presented under the guise of *A Thousand and One Nights* in the above quotation stays connected to

24. Malek Chebel, *Encyclopédie de l'amour en Islam* (Paris: Payot, 1995), 486.

childhood memory and acts as an autobiographical marker. It also releases dream-like accounts and theatricality, as in, for example, a dance imagined through the movement of the narrator's fingers. In this imagined spectacle, each of the five fingers is its own character in a show whose cultural roots arise from the Orient or Asia. According to the narrator, it is a show in which Oriental and Asian tones mingle with one another. Yet even more important for this study on the relationship between surrealism and the Orient, the *Man of Jasmine* takes over from *Nadja* by responding in a constructive way to the asylum experience and opposing it with creativity. The Orient is considered a remedy to all evils, as Breton had claimed two decades prior when he declared: "Today light comes to us from the Orient."

## ORIENTALIST SURREALISM?

Recent studies on surrealism have begun to redefine surrealists with regard to the elitism that marked their movement, "their own orthodoxy" in the words of Henri Béhar, and allow us to reconsider the surrealist movement as a "conglomeration of cultures." By updating our understanding of the role that the surrealists played in the popular culture of the time, we can better situate the importance of the movement in public spaces. Katharine Conley recently documented Robert Desnos' media activities and showed how the surrealists took on a dialogue with public space through the radio. According to Conley, by 1938 Desnos

> developed a dream interpretation program called "La clef des songes," an interactive show that responded on the air to dream narratives sent by individual listeners. . . . In addition to his work writing advertising copy and organizing radio concerts, Desnos was responsible for two memorable nonmusical radio productions: the first reflected his politics, the second his popularization of surrealism.[25]

In the area of social activity, the surrealists' inclination for disguise, fancy dress, and parties is recorded through photographs, portraits, and self-portraits of the group. Yet, these practices fall within the framework of an Orientalist vein that marked the whole vanguard period. Commercial exploitation of *A Thousand and One Nights* continued throughout the 1930s in all spheres of Parisian life. This can be seen,

---

25. Katharine Conley, *Robert Desnos, Surrealism and the Marvelous in Everyday Life*. (Lincoln, NE: Nebraska University Press, 2003), 89, 107.

for example, in the popularity of the gypsy cabaret *Le Shéhérazade* in the ninth arrondissement. In 1934 the Egyptian writer Tawfiq al-Hakin published the play *Chahrazâd*, which was staged at the Comédie-Française in the 1930s. The fashion designer Paul Poiret was the source of these new Orientalist cultural practices, which, from the Belle Époque on, bombarded the world with fashion, fashion photography, costume, and decorative arts. Poiret introduced the turban, the pantaloon, the pantaloon skirts, and the lampshade tunics to Parisian artistic milieus from the 1910s to the 1930s. He also embroidered his creations with Arabic calligraphy and gold thread: "He loved women in the vivid colors and effects of Oriental styles. He imported fabrics from the Middle East and the Far East. He remembered the Persian miniatures."[26] Poiret also began the trend of huge theme parties that continued throughout the vanguard movement, in particular his unforgettable party called "The Thousand and Second Night," which he describes as follows:

> People saw me, in the back of the room, looking like some white-bearded swarthy sultan, holding an ivory handled whip. Surrounding me, on the steps of my throne, all the concubines sprawled out and lascivious, seemed to wait and dread my silence. . . . When my three hundred guests had convened, I stood up and, followed by all my women, I went to the cage of my favorite (Madame Poiret), and set her free.[27]

The cult that the surrealists dedicate to Louise Brooks, the legendary actress remembered for her languorous dances with Alice Roberts in the 1929 film *Pandora's Box*, sheds light on the Orientalist nature of surrealist fantasies. The figure of *la garçonne*[28] incarnated by Louise Brooks is directly inspired by ancient Oriental cultural traditions of cross-dressing, namely the pre-islamic Arabic epic (*Fatah ash-sham*, for example), as well as the erotic Arabo-Persian tradition practiced since Abou Nouwas (762–812), with his *Ghoulamiyâtes* staging love, sung by girls dressed as boys. Thus Louise Brooks contributes to the glance turned toward the Orient and endows the surrealist imagination with Orientalist accents.

Other "big names" of the surrealist repertoire include Marlene

26. Palmer White, *Poiret* (New York: Clarkson N. Potter Inc. Publisher, 1973), 86.
27. Paul Poiret, *En habillant l'époque* (Paris: Éditions Bernard Grasset, 1930), 174–75.
28. The *garçonne* is a girl or young woman with a boyish appearance; she is often defined as an independent woman.

Dietrich who, like Louise Brooks, capitalizes on a similar Orientalist myth in *Der Blaue Engel* (*The Blue Angel*, 1929) and *Cœurs brûlés* (*Morocco*, 1930). This Orientalist myth reoccurs in Hollywood film from its beginnings and persists in Europe between the World Wars. In the movies, it both defines and promulgates the exotic and erotic characteristics of the Orient, place of all promiscuities where the passivity of the Other is revealed. From this perspective, the image of the new and emancipated Western woman, exemplified by Marlene Dietrich in *Cœurs brûlés*, contrasts with the submission of veiled and subordinate Moroccan female characters who shy away at a glance. The myth of the new woman in *Cœurs brûlés* acts as a metaphor to assert and transmit Western modernity. These Orientalist echoes, which reduce the Other to submission and which place themselves at the opposite end of the avant-garde's anticolonial ambitions, are oddly mixed with the construction of the female movie star and the femme fatale.

While the Orient held a privileged place in the surrealist imagination and asserted its presence at the heart of the founding group through the later generations, the surrealists were sometimes seduced by Orientalist trends in their culture. In spite of their numerous interventions against colonization and their obvious effort to internationalize, we can see a conflict between the anticolonial policy of the surrealists and their taste for the popular culture of the period, which was often Orientalist in nature. Although we cannot dub them Orientalists in the sense that their predecessors were, the representation of the Orient in the context of surrealism and the contradictions that it raises underline the deep contradictions, ruptures, and gaps that marked the history of the movement. Could we say, after all, that, in spite of the surrealists' cultural elitism and in spite of their interest in the Orient, they did not escape the clichés of their time and may have been, without a doubt in spite of themselves, both actors in and blind consumers of their popular culture?

# ADAM JOLLES

# The Tactile Turn: Envisioning a Postcolonial Aesthetic in France

The early 1930s witnessed a sudden transformation in the art of the French avant-garde such that its most ardently Leftist members began producing work that appealed first and foremost to tactile perception.[1] Since only those artists either affiliated with or sympathetic to the Parti Communiste Française (PCF) would participate in this transformation, however, this "tactile turn," as I will refer to it, would seem to be implicitly related to the former's political platform. Given that the PCF was concerned at this time above all with the issue of French imperialism, I suggest that this tactile turn accompanied profound ambivalence about the capacity of any aesthetic based exclusively on optical perception to divorce itself from the culture of colonialism.

Taken separately, these theses are not terribly problematic. Any cursory survey of the work produced by the French avant-garde in the early 1930s brings to light the sudden privileging of the tactile, from the movable sculpture of Jean Arp and Alberto Giacometti, to the painted objects of Yves Tanguy, to the monochromatic sand reliefs Picasso made in Juan-le-Pins, to Man Ray's more transparently sensual photographic excurses (Figure 1) of Meret Oppenheim's naked body coated in printing ink, one of which was published in *Minotaure* in 1934 under the title of *l'erotique voilée*.[2] Similarly, concerning the second claim, one need only point to the French Left's complete disavowal

---

1. An earlier version of this article was presented at the Twentieth- and Twenty-First-Century French and Francophone Studies International Colloquium, hosted by the University of Florida, 2005. I am grateful to Katharine Conley, Penny Florence, and Michele H. Richman for their helpful comments on the manuscript.

2. For a study of how surrealism prioritizes the manual with regard to the practice of automatism, see Kirsten H. Powell, "Hands-On Surrealism," *Art History* 20 (Dec. 1997): 516–33.

**YFS 109,** *Surrealism and Its Others,* ed. Katharine Conley and Pierre Taminiaux, © 2006 by Yale University.

*Figure 1.* Man Ray, *Veiled Erotic (Erotique voilée)*, 1933, gelatin-silver print. © 2006 Man Ray Trust/Artists Rights Society (ARS), New York/ADAGP, Paris.

of hybridity around the time of the Exposition Coloniale Internationale of 1931. Those avant-garde icons of the previous decade that had so brilliantly insinuated visual analogies and, by extension, cultural homologies between Europe and its colonies—and I'm thinking here of such emblematic works as Man Ray's *Noire et blanche* (Figure 2) and Hannah Höch's *The Sweet One (Die Sübe)* (Figure 3), both dating to 1926—proved inadequate to the task of even acknowledging, much less addressing, the gross political inequalities between empire and colony that the international fair had brought into such stark contrast.

Taken together, however, these two claims force into view what I take to be the clearly more problematic, but potentially more interesting issue: namely, were these two phenomena related, and if so, how? For if we can demonstrate that the avant-garde's reticence in the 1930s to continue representing colonial motifs in an exclusively visual idiom was motivated by its perception that such an artistic practice was not commensurate with the emerging anti-imperialist discourse, and if we

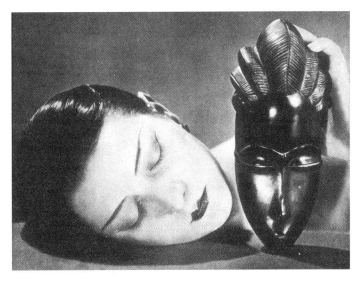

*Figure 2.* Man Ray, *Noire et blanche (Black and White)*, 1926, gelatin-silver print. © 2006 Man Ray Trust/Artists Rights Society (ARS), New York/ ADAGP, Paris.

can explain why a haptic aesthetic might have satisfied the avant-garde's anti-imperialist mandate, we might then be able to show that the appeal a tactile art offered in the 1930s was in fact the promise such a perceptual model held for a postcolonial aesthetic.

This is a tall order, given the limits not only of the documentation we have but of the current orientation of scholarship in this field. It necessitates that we begin to read imagery not only against contemporary ethnographic theory, but also against the political discourses with which that theory was associated, something many scholars have resisted, if only for the absence until recently of concrete evidence.[3] Only the interpenetration of these three domains—visual, ethnographic, and political—will permit us to make sense of the particular iconography associated with French colonialism and that of its various inter-

3. In *Pleine marge* 35 (June 2002), see my article "'Visitez l'exposition anti-coloniale!' Nouveaux éléments sur l'exposition protestataire de 1931" (107–16); Paul Eluard, "La vérité sur les colonies" (117–20); and Louis Aragon, "La vérité sur les colonies, Une salle de l'Exposition anti-impérialiste" (121–28). Eluard and Aragon make clear the emerging distinctions between the Socialist and Communist positions on French colonialism.

*Figure 3.* Hannah Höch, *Die Süße (The Sweet One),* from the series, *From an Ethnographic Museum,* 1926, collage, Museum Folkwang Essen. © 2006 Artists Rights Society (ARS), New York/VG Bild-Kunst, Bonn.

locutors. To approach such a reading, I shall present a brief introduction to the crisis of cultural syncretism that emerged during the Exposition coloniale of 1931, where it became eminently apparent that hybridity of the sort practiced by the avant-garde was being conflated with both the critical methodology of French Socialist ethnography and the visual idiom of French imperialism. I shall follow with a close critical analysis of several emblematic tactile avant-garde works of the early 1930s, and suggest that, in relation to the latter, Tristan Tzara's contemporaneous writings on African art provide something of a theoretical justification for making hapticity a politically viable artistic practice for the Left. Such arguments proved necessary precisely because of the fiercely ideological debates over tactility in the previous decade, when the avant-garde had denounced the privileging of the manual in art as mere artisanship. In the critical writings of Tzara, the tactile is celebrated not as a mere register of craftsmanship or artistic dexterity, but rather as a legitimate index of social value through utility and desire.

By the mid-1920s, the European avant-garde had emphatically embraced precolonial objects not simply for their formal properties but, further, as a means of reinvigorating such increasingly attenuated Western genres as the nude. The spread of this practice was contemporaneous with Picasso's decision in 1924 to sell his *Demoiselles d'Avignon* (1907, Museum of Modern Art, New York) to Parisian collector and surrealist patron Jacques Doucet. While Picasso's brothel offers a formal synthesis of various Iberian heads and "Africanesque" masks atop the nude bodies of the prostitutes avidly displaying themselves therein, the avant-garde of the 1920s approached the question of cultural hybridity with considerably more precision in mind. The most iconic example of the interwar merging of white bodies and African sculpture is Man Ray's photograph *Noire et blanche,* published in the May 1926 issue of *Paris Vogue.* A strikingly stark image, *Noire et blanche* offers only the two figures that correspond to its title: A Baule mask, from the West coast of Africa, and Man Ray's occasional lover, Kiki of Montparnasse. While Kiki languidly rests her powdered head atop the table, she orients the dark, wooden mask vertically to face the camera, drawing obvious formal parallels between the geometric rigidity of its surface patterns and her own severe and stylized countenance. She is also notably displacing her head from her body, surmounting it instead with the mask.

The resulting image, the body of a white woman with the face of an African mask, points to a form of cultural slippage that is essential not only to Man Ray's photograph, but to much work of the 1920s that concerned itself with ethnographic motifs. We see similar homologies between precolonial artifacts and modern Western iconography, for example, being offered by *The Sweet One,* part of the suite of collages Höch executed under the title *From an Ethnographic Museum.* Here, body parts from several fashion plates are spliced together with reproductions of two sculptures from the French Congo then housed in the Musée d'ethnographie du Trocadéro in Paris.[4] As with the Man Ray, the

___

4. For arguments that seek to distinguish between Höch's collages and the photographs of her surrealist contemporaries, see Lora Rempel, who suggests that, where

collage offers the visual culture of two vastly separate civilizations as interchangeable—the modish European flapper loses none of her stylishness in immediate proximity to African tribal objects; likewise, the non-Western artifact is able to signify in some fundamental sense as ritual object despite its conflation with patently European features. There is more than just a little tongue-in-cheek humor in both of these images, manifesting itself in ribald defiance of Western norms of beauty and desirability. By leveling established hierarchies, according to which European cultures are accorded a superior value over those of their colonies, such works presented precolonial artifacts not as subordinates, but rather as equivalents to the imagery produced by the colonizers.

To a generation of French ethnographers, such images embodied through their hybrid imagery not just a potent iconography of cultural de-familiarization, but a veritable method for practicing comparative anthropology. As James Clifford argued in a landmark essay, the experimental group of ethnographers responsible for reinstalling the Trocadéro in 1930—most notably Marcel Griaule, Michel Leiris, and George-Henri Rivière—developed a cross-cultural practice that relied upon the very critical tools with which the surrealists animated their art. So as to emphasize this connection, Clifford labeled this practice "ethnographic surrealism." A collage-like combination of avant-garde creativity and intellectual inquiry, ethnographic surrealism employs the kind of iconographic interchangeability evident in *Noire et blanche* and *The Sweet One*—a dismantling of cultural hierarchies that attacks the familiar, provoking, as Clifford argues, "the irruption of otherness."[5]

---

Höch's work "negates bodily wholeness," the surrealists by contrast "ruptured the internal unity of imaged corporeality but ultimately upheld the ruling tradition of rational, empirical vision and much that is concomitant with that way of seeing as well." Rempel, "The Anti-Body in Photomontage: Hannah Höch's Woman without Wholeness," in *Sexual Artifice: Persons, Images, Politics*, ed. Ann Kibbey, et al. (New York: New York University Press, 1994), 148–70. See also Maria Makela, "By Design: The Early Work of Hannah Höch in Context," in *The Photomontages of Hannah Höch* (Minneapolis: The Walker Art Center, 1997), 70. The reproductions of Congolese sculpture were taken from issues of *Der Querschnitt*, a journal published by the dealer Alfred Flechtheim, dating to 1924 and 1925 (see note 3, *Pleine marge*, 104).

5. James Clifford, "On Ethnographic Surrealism," in *The Predicament of Culture: Twentieth-Century Ethnography, Literature, and Art* (Cambridge, MA: Harvard University Press, 1988), 145–46. See also Denis Hollier, "The Use-Value of the Impossible," *October* 60 (Spring 1992): 3–24; and Jean Jamin, "L'ethnographie mode d'inemploi. De quelques rapports de l'ethnologie avec le malaise dans la civilisation," *Le mal et la*

A central problem with Clifford's thesis, however, is that while the Trocadéro ethnographers of the 1930s may have developed a social science modeled on the aesthetic to which *Noire et blanche* attests, their notion of surrealism failed to evolve historically with the movement itself. The ethnography practiced in the halls of the Trocadéro in 1930 would be far more akin to the Socialist political platform of the subsequent decade, grounded as it was in drawing trans-historic homologies among different ethnic groups and their diverse rituals. Surrealism, by contrast, would push itself in a patently Stalinist direction in 1931, during which time it would emphasize above all the class origins of objects and the present socio-economic context of colonialism. This method, which I have elsewhere referred to as "surrealist ethnography" to distinguish it from Clifford's "ethnographic surrealism," would be simply irreconcilable with the Trocadéro's new Socialist agenda.[6]

The hybridization of colonial and imperial motifs—in the aforementioned cases, between fashionable, European models and hand-crafted, precolonial sculpture—had functioned in the 1920s as a means of reinvigorating both the European avant-garde and the new French science of ethnography. Such cultural imbrication, however, provoked a tremendous amount of anxiety among the surrealists when put to iconoclastic and highly deceptive ends by the sovereign European powers the following decade in the Exposition coloniale. The presence of similar imagery in the imperial spectacle, and in particular the Exposition's uncamouflaged appropriation of cultural hybridity as a signifier of colonialism, would stun surrealism into the tacit realization that such loose allusions to the relationship between colonizer and colonized as suggested by *Noire et blanche* and *The Sweet One* were untenable. An uncompromising anti-imperialist stance, such as that embraced by French Communism, would require either a different iconography, or an altogether different means of engaging with viewers.

Hybridity, as recent studies have demonstrated, was ubiquitous on the fairgrounds of the Exposition coloniale, evident in the exhibition's architecture and the objects displayed in its myriad pavilions. As Patricia Morton has observed in her study of the fair's architecture, the life-size replica of the Angkor Wat complex in Cambodia, the most vis-

---

*douleur,* ed. Jacques Hainard and Roland Kaehr (Neuchâtel: Musée de l'ethnographie, 1986), 45–79.

6. See my forthcoming essay "Surrealist Ethnography: Displaying the Colonies in Interwar France" in *Surrealism Laid Bare, Even* (Manchester: Manchester University Press), ed. Dawn Ades, David Lomas, et al.

ible and highly publicized icon of the Exposition, was itself a pure conflation of indigenous Khmer design and modern Western technology.
While the architectural motifs that adorned its exterior remained faithful to the original, the interior and supporting infrastructure was fabri-
cated from Western materials, such as the glass-block floor that allowed for natural light to illuminate the exhibition halls below.[7] Much
more problematic than the synthesis of imperial motifs and colonial
engineering evident in the fair's architecture were the objects displayed
in the exhibition halls of the Catholic Pavilion. The Communist press
reacted with particular indignation to those icons illustrating the missionary presence in the colonies (Figure 4). Such images had been man-
ufactured largely by indigenous colonial artists, who had adapted their
native styles and sculptural idioms to depict the new social type of the
missionary—identifiable from his European clothing, and the cross
and bible he carries in each hand. Such objects, of a colonial provenance
but endowed with a decidedly Christian iconography that differ-
entiated them in kind from the established traditions in which they had
been modeled, came to be seen as some of the clearest evidence of the
cultural iconoclasm France was practicing on its colonies.[8]

In conflating Western iconography with indigenous art forms or
peoples, such hybrid objects could be considered to be the colonial
counterpart to the two avant-garde images with which I began. Yet, if
such avant-garde works as *Noire et blanche* had been produced with
the goal of advancing a kind of cultural leveling that would lead to the
dismantling of established imperial hierarchies, the kind of hybridity
in evidence on the fairgrounds by contrast had the opposite effect of
reifying those hierarchies. The spectacle at Vincennes would be the
highwater mark of interwar cultural syncretism, and through it French
Communism would learn of the dual danger presented by the kind of
hybridity that elides the politics of colonialism. By funneling the
iconography of colonialism through indigenous forms, state-sanc-
tioned hybridity threatened colonized peoples with cultural icono-

7. Patricia A. Morton, *Hybrid Modernities: Architecture and Representation at the
1931 Colonial Exposition, Paris* (Cambridge, MA: MIT Press, 2000), 6; 195.
8. For reproductions of these objects, see Jean Gallotti, "Les arts indigènes à l'Exposition coloniale," *Art et décoration* 60 (1931), 69–100. For the Communist reaction to
the Catholic Pavilion, see G[eorges]. Cogniat, "Une visite au pavillon des Missions," *L'internationale de l'enseignement* 9 (July 1931): 23, and A. Rossi, "Quand le Christ bénit la
conquête coloniale," *Monde* (29 Aug. 1931): 9–10. For an extended study of such objects,
see Julius E. Lips, *The Savage Hits Back,* trans. by Vincent Benson (New York: University Books, 1966), 164–88.

*Figure 4.* Missionary Statuette, exhibited in the Catholic Pavilion, Pavillon des Missions, Exposition Coloniale Internationale de Paris, 1931.

clasm. It also undermined the effectiveness of the French avant-garde whose work in this vein—no matter how forward-thinking only a decade prior—would now be associated with cultural imperialism. What was at stake in such cross-cultural exchanges, then, was not simply the fate of non-Western rituals and forms, but the very future of Western artistic practice itself. Given the incommensurate weight of imperial and colonial artistic forms, and the State's appropriation of hybridity, the French Left was forced to abandon cultural syncretism as an artistic technique in 1931.

Two separate practices emerged within the avant-garde as a result of this impasse, each of which sought in strikingly different ways to address the growing disparity between imperial and precolonial art. The

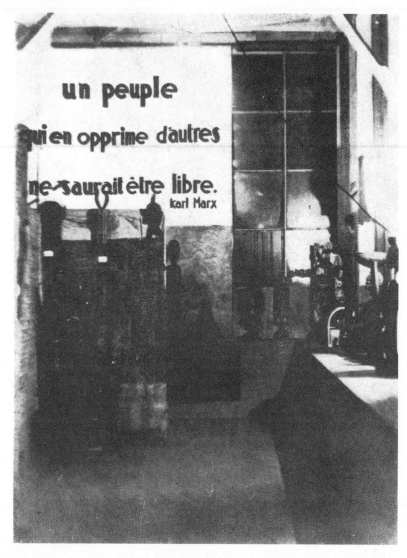

*Figure 5.* Louis Aragon, Installations of pre-colonial and colonial art in *La vérité sur les colonies*, Paris, 1931, *Le surréalisme au service de la révolution* 4 (Dec. 1931).

first such practice was the anti-imperialist exhibition of 1931, *La vérité sur les colonies* [The truth about the colonies], a collaborative effort between the surrealists and the Comintern (Figure 5). Modeling itself on the new Soviet "talking museum" [*samogovoriashchie muzei*], the anti-imperialist exhibition replaces hybridity with an infusion of sup-

plementary text, meant to explicate the historical and socio-economic differences between precolonial artifacts and those objects of a colonial provenance. Adjacent to text panels describing the history of colonialism, a pancolonial selection of indigenous, non-Western artifacts faced off against an array of "European fetishes," whose modeling explicitly revealed the iconography of colonialism. If nothing else, *La vérité sur les colonies* called into question the viability of cultural leveling as an interpretive strategy. To draw homologies, either formal or otherwise, between imperial French objects and precolonial fetishes, its curators argued, would be to ignore the gross political disparities brought into jarring view by the Exposition coloniale.[9]

Despite its rhetorical effectiveness, the anti-imperialist exhibition offered no prescription for avant-garde artistic practice. Indeed, given its emphasis on text as the sole guarantor of truth, its format seems to have precluded artists from participating altogether. Furthermore, in denouncing the by-products of imperialism, *La vérité sur les colonies* left little room for distinguishing between the European fetishes it so unequivocally excoriated and the European avant-garde responsible for its installation. While the anti-imperialist exhibition may have offered an important political retort, then, to both the regressive ethnographic platform espoused by the Exposition coloniale and the more moderate, but politically vacuous humanism presented at the new Trocadéro, its rigid relegation of objects to their place in the socio-economic history of imperialism fostered a great deal of anxiety among its supporters. As a European artist, just how was one to go about practicing an avant-gardism that remained sensitive to the politics of colonialism?

A second artistic practice emerges in the 1930s in response to just this question. A photograph by Man Ray dating to 1932 (Figure 6) provides some of the most eloquent testimony of what we might call the avant-garde's tactile turn. As with his earlier *Noire et blanche*, the photograph contains only two figures in a nondescript space: a white woman and a foreign object. But whereas *Noire et blanche* offers a formal slippage between Kiki's head and the Baule mask, Man Ray's later photograph emphatically privileges the tactile over the optical. Rather than presenting the phallic object in her possession to meet our gaze, his model cradles it sensually against her bared breasts.

The object in Man Ray's later photograph is Giacometti's *Objet désagréable,* part of the series of "objets mobiles et muets" the sculptor illustrated in the journal *Le surréalisme au service de la révolution* in December 1931 (Figure 7). These sculptures are particularly challenging—highly abstract, yet notably intimate in scale, and mounted

---

9. *La vérité sur les colonies* was funded by the Comintern, and at least one of its principal curators, Louis Aragon, had firsthand knowledge of the recent developments in Soviet museology. For more on the latter, see my article "Stalin's Talking Museums," *Oxford Art Journal* 28 (October 2005):429–55. See also K. Grinevich, "Problems of Museum Exposition in the U.S.S.R.," *V.O.K.S.* 2/10–12 (1931), 138–44.

*Figure 6.* Man Ray, *Woman Holding Giacometti's Objet désagréable (Disagreeable Object)*, 1932, gelatin-silver print. © 2006 Man Ray Trust/ Artists Rights Society (ARS), New York/ADAGP, Paris.

on neither pedestals nor a supporting armature. When displayed on the floor well below eye level, as they were at the 1933 Exposition surréaliste at the Galerie Pierre Colle in Paris, their relation to the viewer is unclear and disorienting. As Rosalind Krauss has argued, they point to a noticeable shift in orientation toward horizontality that occurs in Giacometti's oeuvre around 1930.[10]

10. Alberto Giacometti, "Objets mobiles et muets," *Le surréalisme au service de la révolution* 3 (Dec. 1931), 18–19. It should be noted that both the third and fourth issues (the latter of which contained photographs of *La vérité sur les colonies*) were released concurrently. See Rosalind Krauss, "Giacometti," *Primitivism in Twentieth-Century Art: Affinity of the Tribal and the Modern* (New York: Museum of Modern Art, 1984), 503–33; see also Krauss, "No More Play," *The Originality of the Avant-Garde and Other Modernist Myths* (Cambridge, MA: MIT Press, 1985), 43–85. Krauss has sought to align Giacometti's sculpture of this period with George Bataille's contemporaneous development of the concept of "*la bassesse*" (low, or base, materialism), to emphasize the sculptor's distance from orthodox Bretonian surrealism.

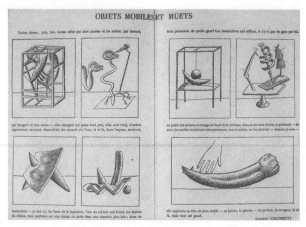

*Figure 7.* Alberto Giacometti, "Objets mobiles et muets," *Le surréalisme au service de la révolution* 4 (Dec. 1931), pp. 18–19.

In the 1931 illustrated catalogue of his works, Giacometti drew a disembodied hand reaching out to touch his *Objet désagréable,* and indeed one of the objects he submitted to the 1933 group show was specifically entitled *Objet désagréable à jeter.* Equally relevant, then, is the extent to which Giacometti emphasized the tactile in these works, and that he did so very much at the expense of the visual.[11] In fact, quite a wide range of objects produced in France in the early 1930s (few of which were horizontal) engaged the issue of hapticity. Works by Man Ray and Valentine Hugo, for example, confirm Giacometti's allusion to the hand as the vital organ for sensual perception, either in the making of marks, as in the case of Man Ray (Figure 1), or in the gesture of the caress, as in the Hugo (Figure 8). Similarly, both Picasso and Meret Oppenheim produced sculptures whose highly textured surfaces seem essential to any sense we might make of them as three-dimensional objects (Figure 9). Finally, along a third axis of work in this vein, one finds an extraordinary series of interactive works—by Jean Arp and Yves

11. I would divide the tactile sculptures Giacometti made after 1930 into three categories: the *sculptures meant to be handled* (the *Objets désagréables, Circuit,* and *Homme, femme, enfant,* all from 1931, and *On ne joue plus* of 1933); *sculptures that take the hand as their subject* (*Main prise* and *Caresse* [*Malgré les mains*] of 1932, *La table* of 1933, and *Mains tenant le vide* [*l'objet invisible*] of 1934); and the *anti-ocular sculpture* (*Pointe à l'oeil* of 1932). See *Alberto Giacometti,* ed. Christian Klemm et al. (New York: The Museum of Modern Art, 2001) for reproductions of these works.

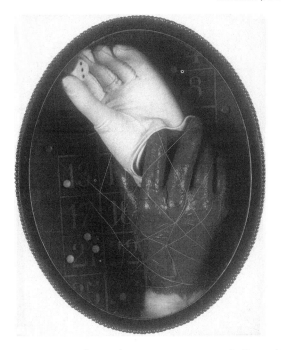

*Figure 8.* Valentine Hugo, *Objet à fonctionnement symbolique (Object with a Symbolic Function)*, 1931, mixed media, private collection. © 2006 Artists Rights Society (ARS), New York/ADAGP, Paris.

Tanguy (Figure 10), most notably. These latter objects involve either the viewer or the curator in the manual assembly of some aspect of the work, and permit alternative configurations.

The choice to move in a patently manual direction seems curious, particularly given the aesthetic debates concerning craftsmanship and manual dexterity that had dominated critical circles the previous decade. When an earlier generation of avant-garde artists had made apparent their preference for questions of *métier*—Giorgio de Chirico foremost among them—the artistic Left had countered by virulently denouncing considerations of technique.[12] In his catalogue essay for the 1930 Exposition des collages at the Galerie Goemans in Paris, entitled "La peinture au défi," Louis Aragon had called for the negation

12. See *On Classic Ground: Picasso, Léger, de Chirico and the New Classicism, 1910–1930* (London: Tate Gallery, 1990).

*Figure 9.* Meret Oppenheim, *Déjeuner en fourrure (Luncheon in Fur)*, 1936, mixed media, Museum of Modern Art, New York. © 2006 Artists Rights Society (ARS), Prolitteris, Zürich.

*Figure 10.* Yves Tanguy, *La certitude du jamais vu (The Certitude of the Never-Seen)*, 1933, oil on board in carved and freestanding wooden frame with gesso, with five carved objects in wood, one with fine hair, The Lindy and Edwin Bergman Collection, The Art Institute of Chicago. © 2006 Estate of Yves Tanguy/Artists Rights Society (ARS), New York.

of *"la personnalité technique,"* or the privileging of the artist's manual skill held in such high esteem in classical art. Such an emphasis, Aragon bemoaned, has today transformed painting into a luxury item, and debased its status to that of a mere "jewel":

> One can imagine a time when the painters who no longer mix their own colors will find it infantile and unworthy to apply the paint themselves and will no longer consider the personal touch, which today still constitutes the value of their canvases, to possess anything more than the documentary interest of a manuscript or autograph. One can imagine a time when painters will no longer even have their color applied by others and will no longer draw. Collage offers us a foretaste of this time.[13]

Gleefully envisioning a future in which art would be liberated equally from the artist's touch and the art market, Aragon dismissed the relevance of tactility in contemporary art, associating it instead with bourgeois painting practices. Collage's appeal, he went on to argue, lay in the ready availability of its raw materials and the ease by which examples could be made by an untrained hand—characteristics that would address his requirement, after Lautréamont, that "the marvelous must be made by all and not by one" (Aragon, *Challenge*, 72). The best collages, he insisted, would be those that were produced spontaneously, without either premeditation or artistic training, whose juxtapositions would suddenly and explosively reveal previously unknown relationships between things.

In the closing chapter of his 1930 book *The Life of Forms in Art*, tellingly entitled "In Praise of Hands," Henri Focillon similarly anticipated a time when traces of the artist's hand would be removed from representation. In contrast to Aragon, however, the art historian deplored this impending passing either through airbrushing or other means of mechanical reproduction. Such was already the case with the photograph, wherein "the hand never intervenes to spread over it the warmth and flow of human life." Coming swiftly to the defense of tactility, Focillon writes eloquently of the need to return the hand to art:

> Knowledge of the world demands a kind of tactile flair. Sight slips over the surface of the universe. The hand knows that an object has bulk, that it is smooth or rough, that it is not soldered to heaven or earth from which it appears to be inseparable. . . . Surface, volume, density and

13. Louis Aragon, "The Challenge to Painting," in *The Surrealists Look at Art*, ed. and trans. Pontus Hulten (Santa Monica, Lapis Press, 1990 [1930]), 55–56.

weight are not optical phenomena. Man first learned about them between his fingers and in the hollow of his palm.[14]

One notable exception to this trend away from the manual had been Paul Gauguin, who had adapted to such indigenous media as pottery, painted wood carvings, and fabric decoration during his years abroad and in the provincial regions of Western France. For Focillon, Gauguin's decision to work in artisanal materials speaks poignantly to his resistance to the depersonalizing effects of modernism, figuring at one and the same time as a mark of his disgust with the "abstraction of money and figures," and a means of "reconquering that eternal antiquity, . . . which possesses and yet escapes him" (170). Focillon makes a telling distinction between the hand of the ethnographer and the "authentic hand" of the "savage" artist. Yet, where Aragon had imagined that the new medium of collage might serve to liberate contemporary artists from the aesthetic constraints of the hand, Focillon, by contrast, completely disavowed contemporary mechanical reproduction in favor of a return to artisanship and its implied connection to "eternal antiquity" (174).

Evidence of a rhetorical shift among Leftist critics in France on the subject of tactility surfaces only after the Exposition coloniale. In a series of articles dating to 1933 broadly surveying the relationship among precolonial sculpture, modern art, and vernacular objects, Tristan Tzara reorients the question of tactility away from the emphasis on manual craftsmanship and more toward utility. In "Primitive Art and Popular Art," for example, an essay published in Stockholm, he argues that despite the sympathy precolonial sculpture has recently elicited from European critics, non-Western art ought not be measured according to Western standards. The main reason for this, he suggests, is that it had been shaped by vastly different perceptual categories, ones that rarely prioritized aesthetics to the extent that their Western counterparts did. Precolonial sculpture, he continues, was conditioned by a different *episteme*, one that above all privileged utility:

> It would be false to assimilate the productions of *art sauvage*, because of their anonymous and mythic character, to that which we improperly refer to as *art populaire*. If the latter, along with *art appliqué*, satisfies itself with a banal look made from visual reminiscences and ingenious

14. Henri Focillon, *The Life of Forms in Art*, trans. Charles B. Hogan and George Kubler (New York: Zone Books, Inc., 1989), 170.

plastic formulations of standardized psychic preoccupations, . . . it must be said that *art sauvage* is characterized above all by the fact of its utility, by its necessity of a superior order, more profoundly human, either religious or social.[15]

Form, Tzara suggests, is born out of need.

In an article published the same year in the journal *Minotaure*, entitled "Concerning a Certain Automatism of Taste," Tzara attempted to clarify the correlation between utility and tactility. Here, he singles out the worn patina evident in certain non-Western objects as a sign of their use-value. Arguing that all proper aesthetic encounters are colored by what he calls "prenatal memories," Tzara seems to be offering a new rationalization for the making of art: "A desire to return to the womb presides over our love for artworks: a feeling of emotional plenitude, of total, absolute, irrational comfort, and of the absence of consciousness and responsibility." Significantly, prenatal memories are not tied to vision, but rather to other sensations—aural, oral, and tactile:

> In the appreciation of the work of art, this prenatal memory, almost always identical among all individuals (tied to the satisfactions offered by substances that can be touched, licked, sucked, crunched, eaten, applied to the skin or the eyelid; warm, dark, damp substances, etc.) is balanced by memories of childhood which permeate in a great variety of ways our tastes and talents for observation, that is, our capacity to specialize and to fixate obsessions.

Objects that have been repeatedly handled, by definition then, respond to a tangible, social need, "a desire which often takes the collective and organized form of some kind of magical use." The effaced patina on these objects is proof, Tzara concludes, that they had "already answered the intrauterine desires of a whole series of individuals." They ought thus be valued neither for the formal arrangements they offer a disinterested viewer, nor for their chronological place in the historical development of cultures, but rather for the spiritual solace they provide a whole society through repetitive, ritualistic use.[16]

A critical component of Tzara's hypothesis is that, despite forsak-

15. Tristan Tzara, "Art primitif et art populaire," *Oeuvres complètes*, vol. 4, ed. Henri Béhar (Paris: Flammarion, 1982), 513, my translation.

16. Tzara, "D'un certain automatisme du goût," *Minotaure*, 3–4 (1933), 81–84; trans. by Pontus Hulten as "Concerning a Certain Automatism of Taste," in *The Surrealists Look at Art*, ed. Hulten (Santa Monica: Lapis Press, 1990), 210.

ing all sensorial experience in favor of the visual, humanity remains bound to an intrauterine account of the world that originated with tactile representations. Thus, all encounters between consciousness and the external world—including those that involve art—are marked by the urge to return to that origin: "To appreciate a work of art, man needs to verify the previous tactile experiences associated with it, experiences which are the concrete form of intrauterine representations. It is clear that this practice perfects the process of transference by which tactile and gustatory sensations are experienced *visually*" (Tzara, 210). Tzara's point in developing this elaborate theory of tactility in relation to non-Western art was, of course, to offer a prescription for both contemporary artistic production and ethnographic inquiry—an antidote to the crisis of cultural syncretism and an alternative model to the Trocadéro ethnographers. Regarding the former, he suggests that we strive "to create rationally objects that are necessary not only from the point of view of their functional utility, but also—and above all—from that of the secret demands of psychic representations" (212). In reference to the latter, his brief meditation on the proper classification and display of ethnographic objects is a fascinating extension of his theory. Rather than devoting themselves to the categorization of series, Tzara argues, ethnographic museums ought to "facilitate the study of the desires that are themselves the basis of customs and the stable element throughout their formations. Beside primitive objects will be ranged those which have replaced them over time, in response to the same subconscious demands of human desires."[17]

Tzara's consideration of tactile registers, or what we might call the index of utility, remains to be carefully distinguished from the analytical model developed by the Trocadéro ethnographers writing for *Documents*. I suspect a distinction might be found in the complicated category of desire. Such recent interlocutors of surrealism as Margaret Cohen and Hal Foster have sought to clarify the overdetermined value of this term in the 1930s by comparing surrealism to the contempora-

---

17. Tzara would be the co-curator of the Exposition surréaliste at the Galerie Pierre Colle in June of 1933, wherein the surrealists first unveiled their tactile objects. In a critical review of the show, Roger Caillois expanded upon Tzara's understanding of utility when he observed, "it is clear that the utilitarian function of an object never completely justifies its form. The object," he continues, "always goes beyond the instrument. It is thus possible to discover an irrational residue in every object, motivated . . . by the inventor's or the technician's unconscious representations." See Roger Caillois, "Le décor surréaliste de la vie," *Documents 33* [Brussels] 5 (1933): 16–17.

neous writings of Freud and interwar applications of Marxist theory (in the work of Walter Benjamin, for example).[18] While such inquiries have helped enormously to illuminate the theoretical armatures of psychoanalysis, Gothic Marxism (to borrow Cohen's term), and avant-gardism, I am more inclined at this point to turn to a much more recent development in psychoanalytic studies for a theoretical analogue to surrealism's tactile turn, one that would preserve the activist spirit behind the new aesthetic.

Luce Irigaray's critical rereading of Freud on female sexuality, "Ce sexe qui n'en est pas un" (1977), and her slightly later "Fécondité de la caresse: lecture de Lévinas" (1983) each negotiates, in its own way, the issue of touch—particularly the *caress*—as a key to the phylogenetic constitution of femininity. Countering the Freudian paradigm, which notoriously reduces woman to a state of lack, her sexual organs as atrophied, and her ego as animated by penis envy, Irigaray advances in contrast a radical theory predicated upon the plurality of female sexuality and the auto-eroticism it is uniquely capable of implementing (through the continuous contiguity of the two lips of the vagina). It is precisely the exercising of feminine auto-eroticism that, for Irigaray, holds the revolutionary promise of liberation from the masculine commodification of women's bodies, an idea that broadly resonates with the surrealist attempt to locate a postcolonial aesthetic in the haptic. So too, her later advocacy of the primal gesture, the nonmaternal, nondiscursive caress as the sole means of guaranteeing the equable encounter with radical alterity (and the occasional transcendence of its thresholds) offers fertile terrain for converging feminist theory with postcolonial ideology.[19]

Skeptics should rightly balk at the suggestion that any single perceptual domain, tactile or otherwise, might satisfy the avant-garde anticolonial imperative at the beginning of the 1930s, especially among the surrealists. Indeed, it was precisely because imperial French art had so aggressively emphasized the optical at the expense of all other sensations that such a problem had emerged in the first place. And Tzara's

18.  Margaret Cohen, *Profane Illumination: Walter Benjamin and the Paris of Surrealist Revolution* (Berkeley: University of California Press, 1993); Hal Foster, *Compulsive Beauty* (Cambridge, MA: MIT Press, 1993); see also David Lomas, *The Haunted Self: Surrealism, Psychoanalysis, Subjectivity* (New Haven: Yale University Press, 2000).

19.  Luce Irigaray, "Ce sexe qui n'en est pas un," in *Ce sexe qui n'en est pas un* (Paris: Éditions de Minuit, 1977); see also, "Fécondité de la caresse: lecture de Levinas," *Exercises de la patience* 5 (Spring 1983): 119–37.

appeal to a criticism dependent in part on Western psychology under-mines his effort to broaden the cultural basis of aesthetic inquiry. Nev-ertheless, preliminary evidence suggests that at the very least the Com-munist avant-garde perceived a way out of the artistic impasse caused by imperialism by making art that was meant to be anything but looked at. It would be work that would by necessity require an entirely differ-ent analytic and descriptive vocabulary—one that could bring to life the fetishistic, totemic, idolatrous, and/or ritualistic aspects of these objects (to name just a few of the obvious relevant categories). Perhaps the recent reemergence of this vocabulary in contemporary critical dis-course points to the surrealists' belated success in reorienting Western aesthetic practice. The extent to which this proved in any way to be a *viable* model for a postcolonial aesthetic practice, however, is an alto-gether different matter.

JONATHAN P. EBURNE

# Antihumanism and Terror: Surrealism, Theory, and the Postwar Left

In the inaugural issue of the postwar surrealist magazine *Le surréal-isme, même* (1956), the young surrealist writer Alain Joubert printed a brief anecdote in the "Notes" section. The anecdote, entitled "So Be It" ["Ainsi soit-il"], provides a humorous commentary on both France's postwar colonial situation and the politics of the surrealists and their fellow leftist intellectuals. Joubert writes:

> In the equatorial jungle lives a tribe of Indians, the Aucas, who have al-ways refused any relationship with whites, in order to avoid the civi-lizing gangrene.
>
> Last January, however, a small team of missionaries decided to go teach the Gospel to these last representatives of the Paleolithic era. A group of five, pure-hearted Americans, in whose midst could be distin-guished a rugby player and a former paratrooper, thought they could successfully approach the Aucas by offering them gifts of the "little-alu-minum-kettle-filled-with-brightly-colored-buttons" kind.
>
> This was to miscalculate how little affection the Indians bore to-ward whites in general and, it seems, toward "God's messengers" in par-ticular. No sooner had they completed their settlement near the village, which lay on a branch of the Curaray river, than the evangelists found themselves in the presence of a group of Aucas who, with the help of a few deftly-thrown spears, soon managed to restore the forest to its ini-tial purity.
>
> I would say, as far as I'm concerned, that I can only agree with this definitive way of ridding oneself of such undesirable visitors.[1]

The matter-of-fact tone of Joubert's anecdote of preemptive anticolo-nial violence is hardly accidental. The story itself is historically accu-

1. Alain Joubert, "Ainsi soit-il," *Le surréalisme, même* 3 (3rd trimester, 1956): 152–53. Translations throughout this article are mine unless otherwise noted.

**YFS 109,** *Surrealism and Its Others,* ed. Katharine Conley and Pierre Taminiaux, © 2006 by Yale University.

rate, as are the Aucas themselves; yet both Joubert's title, "So Be It," and even the French valences of the name "Aucas"—a homonym for "OK" as well as for the open-ended causality of "au cas" [in the event that]—overdetermine the anecdote's appeal to the "naturalness" of returning the jungle to its original purity. In fact, to translate Joubert's French more accurately, what he actually writes is that the assassination of the missionaries "gives back to the forest its initial purity." The "purity" here, in other words, does not designate an irredeemable state of virgin primitivism but a state of equilibrium that can be exchanged, preserved, or taken away.

Joubert's report bears scrutiny because its microcosm of anticolonial violence self-consciously condenses the argument of Aimé Césaire's 1955 *Discourse on Colonialism,* an essay very much at the forefront of the surrealist imagination in the 1950s. Joubert's anecdote appropriates a real news item to illustrate Césaire's famous insistence that colonial relations not only impose the very notion of "the primitive" upon so-called primitive societies, but, in doing so, also violently disrupt the "harmonious and viable economies adapted to the indigenous population."[2] André Breton likewise appeals to Césaire's *Discourse* in a speech reprinted in the opening pages of the same issue of *Le surréalisme, même.* Breton's speech, "For the Defense of Liberty," was delivered in April 1956 to an organization of leftist intellectuals mobilizing against France's military suppression of colonial uprisings in Algeria, as well as against de Gaulle's incarceration of left-wing French reporters who printed dissenting views. In the speech, Breton explicitly invokes Césaire's diatribe against colonialism as a violent disruption of indigenous culture, closing with a number of citations from Césaire's text, whose distribution he calls a "spiritual weapon *par excellence.*"[3]

But what is a spiritual weapon? And to what extent does Breton's notion of a spiritual weapon imply the kind of violence Joubert's article reports? Joubert's "So Be It" condones anticolonial violence—one might even say Terror, in the historical sense of an organized transformation of principles into homicidal action—in a way that neither Cé-

2. Aimé Césaire, *Discourse on Colonialism* (1955), trans. Joan Pinkham. (New York: Monthly Review Press, 1972), 43.

3. André Breton, "Discours au meeting 'Pour la Défense de la Liberté,' Salle des Horticulteurs, le 20 avril 1956," *Le surréalisme, même* 1 (3rd trimester 1956); rpt. *Perspective cavalière,* ed. Marguerite Bonnet (Paris: Gallimard, 1970), 126. See also Jean Schuster's "Open Letter to Aimé Césaire," *Le surréalisme, même* 1 (1956): 146–47.

saire nor Breton make explicit in their more overtly political speeches.[4] The question of whether or not Joubert's Aucas Indians reduce the subtleties of anticolonial political theory to a kind of terrorism or even ethnic cleansing is a question his anecdote defiantly poses, since to claim the innocence of the Aucas would be to misread the story entirely: the assassination of the missionaries is a rejection of the very position of "innocence"—in the sense of both "primitives" and "dupes"—that the Aucas are trying to avoid. Joubert thus articulates the problem of violence at stake in such theories of insurrectional politics, in portraying anticolonial violence as something more than merely a "spiritual weapon." But what happens when the revolutionary group is no longer a small tribe of Amazonian natives, but the colonized peoples of Algeria, a group of militants, or a former revolutionary state like the Soviet Union? This was a question that would become one of the most pivotal in postwar French and francophone intellectual debate, not only with regards to the politics of surrealism, but with regards to the nature of anticolonial struggle, and even Revolution itself, more broadly.

The ties between surrealism's politics and the problem of terrorist violence briefly became a public issue once more in 2001, in the wake of 9/11. Recalling the surrealist movement's violently anticolonial and anti-Western rhetoric, especially visible during the 1920s and 1930s, the prominent French curator Jean Clair recently excoriated the movement for its resemblance to al-Qaida. In a newspaper editorial published in December 2001, Clair juxtaposed the destruction of the World Trade Center with Louis Aragon's 1925 rant against the "white buildings" of New York City, suggesting a causal (rather than merely analogical) relationship between fundamentalist terrorism and the interwar European avant-garde. In making this juxtaposition, Clair contends that "the surrealist ideology never stopped hoping for the death of an America it saw as materialist and sterile, and for the triumph of an Orient that served as the repository for the values of the mind."[5] More than simply a historical coincidence, Clair argues that surrealism's anti-Western and pro-"Oriental" ideology helped "prepare the minds" of European civilization—yet prepared them not for revolution, but for an antihumanism complicit with the forms of totalitari-

4. A more direct interrogation of anticolonial violence would later become the focus of the first chapters of Frantz Fanon's *The Wretched of the Earth*, published a few years later in 1961, at the height of the Algerian war.

5. Jean Clair, *Du surréalisme considéré dans ses rapports au totalitarisme et aux tables tournantes* (Paris: Mille et une nuits, 2003), 118.

anism and state terror that would follow, from Stalinist purges to the Holocaust.

Clair's polemic is not, however, an attack on the surrealist movement's actual political thinking, as represented in the many tracts, pamphlets, and speeches the surrealists produced throughout the movement's history, but on its avant-garde rhetoric. Indeed, Clair's own charge of surrealism's complicity in 9/11—a rhetorical gesture *par excellence*—is a reaction, he claims, against the ideological stakes of surrealism's own intensified rhetoric, whose insults and violent polemics "are no different from those found in the fiery attacks of the fascist leagues or, on the other side of the political spectrum, those soon to be addressed to the 'mad dogs' in the Moscow trials. They signal an era" (Clair, 124–25). Violent rhetoric produces violent action, Clair insists; and because surrealism spoke, and because its rhetoric thus served as the conduit between its artistic practices and the political sphere, surrealist appeals to violence and to the dissolution of Western humanistic ideals cannot safely be viewed as autonomous artistic utterances. In "seeking to conflate *vita contemplativa* and *vita politica*," Clair argues, the movement's members become as subject to judgment and condemnation as any member of a political party (195; 65).

Clair's argument against the totalitarian and terrorist consequences of avant-garde rhetoric is hardly a recent invention; it recalls the situation in which French intellectuals found themselves after World War II, as they struggled to forge a political platform in the wake of National Socialism, Stalinism, and the increasing conservatism of de Gaulle's France during the Cold War. Clair's book, in fact, rehearses the anxieties of a large body of French writing published in the late 1940s and early 50s; these studies likewise attacked the "totalizing" and terrorist tendencies in communism, in Marxism, and even in Hegelian philosophy—ideological and philosophical systems that had significantly oriented avant-garde practices between the wars, and most heroically during the Resistance. Among the most significant of such works are Maurice Merleau-Ponty's 1947 book *Humanism and Terror*, and Albert Camus's 1951 book *The Rebel*, each of which uses the lesson of the prewar Moscow trials as an occasion to interrogate the opposition between liberal values and the political tactics of violence, propaganda, and terror used to implement them. Camus's book, in particular, attacks "revolutionary" movements—whether communism, fascism, or surrealism—for becoming murderous, in principle, precisely at the moment when their commitment to action makes its rhetoric transparent and "demands the suspension of freedom." At this point, Camus writes, "terror, on a grand or small scale, makes its appearance to consummate the revolution."[6] As with Clair's critique, written in the aftermath of 9/11, the postwar French discourse about the problems of avant-gardism and revolutionary politics was deeply concerned by the tendency for the utopian promises of insurrectional movements to become conflated with, or even implicated, in the forms of state terror that recent world events had revealed to be, according to Camus, the "logical conclusion of inordinate technical and philosophical ambitions (Camus, 177).

The surrealist movement's political thinking of the 1950s offers a useful platform for addressing such concerns precisely because it confronted the ethical and epistemological stakes of contemplating violence as a political weapon. Surrealist thinking of the 1950s, as I will demonstrate in what follows, shared with existentialism and anticolonialism a theoretical project that strove to assimilate the spiritual or intellectual liberation promised by avant-gardism with the practical liberation of insurrectional politics. Yet it sought to do this in ways that avoided the formalism, and thus the systematic violence, of "totalitarian" ideological platforms, whether communist, fascist, or even humanist. In particular, the surrealist movement's post-World War II debates with existentialism, as well as with its own theoretical and "philosophical" tendencies, were especially sensitive to the distinctions—or the lack thereof—between leftist revolutionary violence and murderous crime. Surrealism deliberately and concertedly abandoned the traditional cultural position of avant-gardism, instead positioning itself within the broader, antihumanist framework of leftist theory. In place of a rigid ideological platform or a distinctive set of artistic and political practices, the surrealists of the 1950s developed a collective strategy for thinking about political responsibility that short-circuited the "barbarous" rigidity of terrorism itself, that is, of Terror.

The title of the glossy new surrealist magazine that appeared in 1956, *Le surréalisme, même,* articulates the movement's peculiar cultural

---

6. Albert Camus, *The Rebel: An Essay on Man in Revolt,* trans. Anthony Bower (New York: Knopf, 1954), 77. See also Jules Monnerot's *Sociologie du communisme* (1949), translated as *The Sociology and Psychology of Communism* (Boston: Beacon Press, 1953), which notably compares Communism to Islam and medieval Christianity, insofar as its converts "were able to attack in the name of the true Faith the very societies which had brought the Faith to them" (15). According to Benjamin Péret, Monnerot's book was an unacknowledged source for Camus's essay.

and political situation during the mid-1950s. For one, the title's self-re-flexivity ["surrealism itself"] alludes to recent attacks on the movement's datedness, which claimed that surrealism had become institutionalized and solipsistic. At the same time, the title's allusion to Marcel Duchamp's similarly reflexive *Large Glass* from 1923, *La mariée mise à nu par ses célibataires, même,* advertised not only that Duchamp's works would feature heavily in the magazine, but also that his theories of reflection and reflexivity were significant to 1950s surrealism. Duchamp's notion that a work of art comes into being through the aporia of judgment and inter-pretation that takes place between the art object and its spectators—the notion that "it's the spectators that make paintings"—would serve as sur-realism's answer to existentialist phenomenology.

The idea that the surrealism of 1956 was looking back to the surre-alism of the 1920s did not, however, represent a mere retrenchment within the movement's earlier aesthetic principles. The editorial pref-ace to *Le surréalisme, même,* in response to its question of "A new sur-realist journal! Why?," wishes to dissuade the movement's adherents and critics alike from falling into the trap of thinking that surrealism was merely about itself, a style or a school of thought. As the preface states, the magazine seeks "To forestall that current confusion brought about, for unprepared minds, by the increasing profusion of ventures whose aim is artificially to reproduce the climate of surrealism with the intention of promoting, both towards and against it, strangeness for the sake of strangeness, humour for humour's sake, or any other solu-tion just as aberrant as that of art for art's sake."[7] The means for pre-venting or forestalling such confusion, I'd like to suggest, was for the group to remind itself, and especially its more recent members, of the conditions that determined surrealism's political turn during the 1920s. As Breton's speech for the "Defense of Liberty" meeting makes explicit, the movement's political engagement in the mid-1920s was a direct response to France's military suppression of Abd-el-Krim's anti-colonial insurgency in the Rif section of Morocco. In a postwar era scarred not only by the horrors of fascism but also by Stalinist invasion and France's current mobilization against Algerian and Vietnamese in-dependence, Breton's reminder about the 1920s locates the impetus for surrealist politics within its support for decolonization. In other words,

7. "Note for *Le surréalisme, même,*" *Le surréalisme, même* 1 (1956), in *Surrealism Against the Current: Tracts and Declarations,* ed. and trans. Michael Richardson and Krzysztof Fijalkowski (London: Pluto Press, 2001), 51.

the communist party affiliation that promised, for several years in the late 1920s, to provide a concrete means for political intervention, had been only a temporary means, rather than the impetus or end, of surrealism's political commitment. The movement's subsequent years of debate with and ultimate rejection of orthodox communism had clouded this earlier commitment to decolonization. Ever since the early 1930s, and increasingly after the Moscow trials of 1936 and 1937, the surrealists loudly excoriated Stalinism as a form of state Terror not only complicit with capitalism and fascism, but coextensive with their imperial aims as well.

As the young surrealist writer Nora Mitrani put it more broadly, under such conditions the true murderers were no longer individual criminals but the systematic organizations that committed violence under the aegis of principles, laws, or the state. As Mitrani writes, "the collective massacres of these last few years have proven only too well that the crime of passion had ceased to be a solitary and magnificent mystery, but instead organized itself, crumbled into office files, into racial laws, faded into concepts of the Good and the Honorable."[8] Mitrani's ironic appeal to the mystery and romance of old-fashioned crimes of passion is not a real expression of nostalgia, of course, but instead an accusation of the facility with which acts of state terror or even genocide conceal their criminality behind the abstractions of administration and humanistic principles. The organizations Mitrani and the surrealists reviled, in other words, gave terror and murder an alibi.

Oscillating between Trotskyite and neo-anarchist political affiliation throughout the 1950s, surrealism's postwar project was oriented toward defending revolution and intellectual freedom against the ideological and state apparatuses that worked to suppress it. Surrealism's project was no longer avant-garde in the sense that it sought to *incite* revolutionary thought or action through its works, but, we might say, almost progressivist insofar as it sought both to defend and to extend such thought and action as it happened.

Two essays by the poet Benjamin Péret dramatize this adjustment. The first, a hopeful essay published in the first issue of *Le surréalisme, même*, "Is this the dawn" ["Est-ce l'aube"], praises the Algerian insurgency alongside proletarian uprisings against communist rule in Poznan and in East Berlin, as well as student demonstrations in Prague and

8. Nora Mitrani, "De l'objectivité des lois," *Le soleil noir* 2, "Le temps des assassins" (June 1952). Rpt. *Rose au coeur violet* (Terrain Vague, 1988), 49.

Budapest, as evidence that "we are witnessing the first attempts of the international proletariat to seize back the direction of its struggles, in rejecting the dead weight of traditional organizations."[9] A second essay, published a few months later in the second issue of the magazine, chronicles the bloody suppression of the Hungarian revolution by Russian troops in 1956 as the final phase of Stalinism's evolution, which, Péret charges, "rose from social strata foreign to the revolution and sought nothing other than to profit from the possibilities granted by the new revolutionary order."[10] Péret's essays, written after years of travel between Spain, France, Mexico, and Brazil as a militant Trotskyite, are by far the most adamant surrealist writings in their criminalization of the Soviet Union and the French republic as terrorist states. Yet Péret nevertheless shared with the other 1950s surrealists, as well as with many anticolonial political theorists, including Jean-Paul Sartre and Frantz Fanon, the notion that colonial and imperial power was responsible for the revolts their oppression provoked, and that anticolonial violence was justifiable as a form of self-defense. Moreover, the military or ideological suppression of such revolts by the powers that instigated them became, in turn, a kind of double crime.[11]

Given their hostility toward the systematic violence, whether explicit or implicit, of state apparatuses, the surrealists would seem to be in concert with the numerous attacks on Stalinism that proliferated after the war, especially following the publication of Arthur Koestler's novel *Darkness at Noon*, which appeared in French as *Le zéro et l'infini*, in 1945. Yet whereas the surrealists would share the Left's contempt for, or at least discouragement with, the fate of Bolshevism under Stalin, they were skeptical of the way other French intellectuals modeled their broader critiques of revolution and terror after the Soviet example. Koestler's fictionalized account of the Moscow trials notably cites the trials as the culminating moment at which, he writes, "Revolutionary theory had frozen to a dogmatic cult, with a simplified, easily graspable catechism, and with No. 1 [i.e. Stalin] as the high priest celebrating the mass."[12] For Koestler's protagonist, Rubashov,

9. Benjamin Péret, "Est-ce l'aube," *Le surréalisme, même* 1 (1956): 156.
10. Péret, "Calendrier accusateur," *Le surréalisme, même* (1957): 59.
11. See Péret, "Assez de tortures," *Le surréalisme, même* 3 (Autumn 1957): "Every colonial power is thus responsible for the revolts its oppression provokes and for the inevitable violences they include, without which such revolts are admissible in spite of themselves."
12. Arthur Koestler, *Darkness at Noon* (1941), trans. Daphne Hardy (New York: Time Incorporated, 1962), 143.

the experiences of imprisonment and examination put on trial both Rubashov's own complicity with the "dogmatic cult" of Stalinism he had recently been serving, and also the "Revolutionary theory" itself. For what comes flooding back to Rubashov during his sleep-deprived days of interrogation is the question that would be posed by many French intellectuals in the years after the war: at what point did the Revolution's historical logic of necessity stifle and overwhelm the lives of the human subjects it was designed to liberate? As Rubashov muses, the object of revolution may be the abolition of suffering, but the removal of suffering has turned out to be possible only at the price of an enormous increase in suffering. "Was such an operation justified?" Rubashov asks, to which he responds: "Obviously it was, if one spoke in the abstract of 'mankind'; but, applied to 'man' in the singular . . . the real human being of bone and flesh and blood and skin, the principle led to absurdity" (Koestler, 206). Rubashov's conundrum—and especially his appeal to the basic humanism that his party activities had so long repressed—is the starting-point of Maurice Merleau-Ponty's 1947 study of Koestler's implications, *Humanism and Terror.* For Merleau-Ponty, the problem exceeds merely the "absurd" contradiction between the abolition of suffering in theory and the increase of suffering in practice, to comprise the paradoxes of revolutionary movements more broadly.

Merleau-Ponty's titular allusion to the French Terror of 1793 suggests precisely that the question of revolutionary policy, and the question of a revolution's future, is intrinsic to radical thought's relationship to what he calls "the ambiguity of history." Since, Merleau-Ponty writes, we are not spectators of a closed history but in fact actors in an open history, "our *praxis* introduces the element of construction rather than knowledge as an ingredient of the world, making the world not simply an object of contemplation but something to be transformed."[13] Because there can be no absolute knowledge of historical ends, political action is based only on probabilistic calculation. That is, the justification for any revolutionary *ends* is based on a historical wager that renders every revolution a matter of force and violence. For Merleau-Ponty, this is a broader problem than that of the violence within Stalinism alone; indeed, he returns to the violence intrinsic in Western Humanism itself: "How do we answer an Indochinese or an Arab who

13. Maurice Merleau-Ponty, *Humanism and Terror: An Essay on the Communist Problem,* trans. John O'Neill (Boston: Beacon Press, 1969), 92.

reminds us that he has seen a lot of our arms but not much of our humanism?" (Merleau-Ponty, 175). For Merleau-Ponty, the Terror of History itself, in framing violence as part of any historical decision, demands that we seek a new humanism in order to preserve the possibility of revolution. He defines this new humanism as a "harmony with ourselves and others, in a word, truth, not only in *a priori* reflection and solitary thought but through the experience of concrete situations and in a living dialogue with others apart from which internal evidence cannot validate its universal right" (187). This radically contingent form of dialogic social reorganization forms the core of Merleau-Ponty's understanding of existentialism, the conception of the human world as an open or unfinished system that posits "the experience of the other person as an alter ego" (187).

Albert Camus, in *The Rebel*, published four years later in 1951, extends Merleau-Ponty's problematic even further. In a way that would soon provoke the disapproval of the surrealists, Camus isolates revolt as a Cartesian and Kantian principle of humanism through which the archetypal rebel—for Camus, a "slave" who says "no" to the master— risks his life "for the sake of a common good which he considers more important than his own destiny. . . . He acts, therefore, in the name of certain values which are still indeterminate but which he feels are common to himself and to all men" (Camus, 21). The critical difference between Merleau-Ponty's existentialist humanism and Camus's "man in revolt" lies in each author's conception of the ideological and historical forces that pervert the historical wager of "revolt" and transform it into forms of Terror and murder that exterminate the very values it stood for. Whereas Merleau-Ponty strives to rescue Marxist and revolutionary theory from Terror by arguing that Marxism advocates a dialectical process of knowledge and praxis, rather than imposing absolutes, Camus instead implicates virtually the entire intellectual genealogy of revolutionary thought in France as bearing the seeds of Terror within its own logic. Indeed, *The Rebel* pathologizes not only Marx, Nietzsche, and Hegel, but also Sade, Baudelaire, Lautréamont, and the surrealists. Unlike Jean Clair, though, Camus does not so much accuse such figures as being the cause of totalitarianism and terror as he demonstrates their complicity with the same dynamic of corruption that transforms idealism into terror. This dynamic describes any form of thought that subjects man, as Camus writes, to a formal principle:

> Historical thought was to deliver man from subjection to a divinity; but this liberation demanded of him the most absolute subjection to his-

torical evolution. Then man takes refuge in the concept of the permanence of the party in the same way that he formerly prostrated himself before the altar. That is why the era which dares to claim that it is the most rebellious that has ever existed only offers a choice of various types of conformity. The real passion of the twentieth century is servitude.[14]

The real passion of the twentieth century was not, in other words, the suppression or repression of freedom, but the servitude and conformity of so-called revolutionaries. What disturbed the surrealists most about Camus's formulation was the tendency for his abstraction of Terror to conflate the revolutionary and the terrorist, and, in doing so, to place the onus of historical responsibility upon the oppressed, upon Camus's "slave" who says no.

In their extensive polemical exchanges with Camus in the leftist press, the surrealists expressed shock toward Camus's conclusions, in spite of their general consensus with his argument that Terror was an ideological as well as a historical phenomenon. *The Rebel* strives to isolate a form of revolt that does not become an immoderate mechanism of violence and murder, by opposing to "revolution in the name of power and of history" a new rebellion, "in the name of moderation and of life" (272). Breton, however, considered such an attempt to introduce a revolt "emptied of its impassioned content" to be a logical contradiction. As he writes in a critique of Camus's book, "Can revolt be both itself and mastery, the perfect domination of itself, at the same time?"[15] Breton criticizes Camus's overall logic for presuming a constant and irrevocable historical progression of revolutionary thought from "revolt" to terror. That is, not only did Camus abstract "revolt" from the recourse to violence that rendered it possible in the first place, but Camus's reading of historical figures like Marx, Hegel, Lautréamont, and the surrealists presupposed within their "revolutionary" writing the conclusions of servitude and complicity he wished to derive from them in advance. Camus did not allow the possibility for truly revolutionary thought to disrupt its own tendency toward dogmatism.

14. Albert Camus, *The Rebel*, 203–4. As Debarati Sanyal argues in a recent study of Camus's work, the novelty of *The Rebel* lies in its "treatment of terror as a formal principle that could be deployed in the distinct fields of philosophy, politics, and aesthetics." See Debarati Sanyal, "Broken Engagements," *Yale French Studies* 98 (2000): 32.

15. André Breton, "Dialogue avec Aimé Patri à propos de "l'Homme révolté" d'Albert Camus," *Oevres Complètes*, vol. 3, ed. Marguerite Bonnet et al. (Paris: Gallimard, 1999), 1054.

As Benjamin Péret explains in his contribution to a collection of surrealist responses to *The Rebel*, in a language that resonates strongly
with 1950s surrealism's theories of intellectual and artistic practice,
"the instrument"—and here Péret is talking about philosophical influences, but could just as easily be talking about violence—"is neutral;
it's only the use one makes of it that bestows dignity or indignity. A pen
can just as well serve to write a poem as a police report."[16] It is still the
responsibility of the revolutionary to resist the dogmatism of concepts
and to short-circuit the administrative formalism that leads to ideological and genocidal forms of Terror.

For the surrealists, though, this responsibility to resist the perver-
sion of revolutionary theory into Terror did not demand a return either
to Merleau-Ponty's existentialist intersubjectivity or to Camus's
"moderation and life" as necessary forms of humanist mediation. "I
formally contest," writes Gérard Legrand in the pages of *Le surréalisme, même*,

> that surrealism *is* a humanism (or a "sur-humanism") at all. I would say
> that liberty can think itself and even conceptualize itself without tak-
> ing into account *the human,* that hybrid of medieval Thomism, post-
> Renaissance skepticism (Montaigne) and the "open" morals of univer-
> sity skepticism. Surrealism is not a philosophy: it is the crossroads, the
> meeting-place of several philosophies that have significance only in
> mutually completing themselves before the flaming hearth of poetry.
> But if it has been able to coincide, under precise conditions, with con-
> temporary humanisms for the defense of interests and values belonging
> to "the mind," this is not because man was the bearer of these values;
> in my opinion it's for these values, and for the mind itself.[17]

As Legrand's essay suggests, surrealism posited its own form of mediation—indeed, the group's very reason for existence, especially
throughout the 1950s, might be described as its desire to organize the

16. Benjamin Péret, "Le revolté du dimanche" (1952), rpt. *Oeuvres complètes*, vol. 7,
ed. Association des amis de Benjamin Péret (Paris: José Corti, 1995), 180. As Péret writes
of the fate of Marxian thought elsewhere in his article, "Marx is a principal element in
the revolutionary and socialist thought of the past century. What matters is submitting
him to the critique to which he submitted his predecessors and contemporaries, in order
that the living elements of them all . . . might find their place in a theory better adapted
to the necessities of our time." Péret does not deny a link between Marxist thought and
Stalinism, but that link is that between "the meat and the fly that spoils it, of liberty and
the gendarme, of the revolution and the counter-revolution" (178).

17. Gérard Legrand, "Le surréalisme est-il une philosophie?" *Le surréalisme, même*
1 (1956): 144.

relationship between political revolution and art in a way that would short-circuit the orthodoxies Merleau-Ponty and Camus describe.

Such an organization, however, demanded a redefinition not only of the relationship between political thought and aesthetics—a relationship the surrealists configured as a dialectic—but also of the nature of poetry and art themselves as something other than a means for human expression. In place of a traditional understanding of art as representation, the surrealists posited the role of art within political thought as being constituted within and by the dialectic of interpretation that takes place between the object and its spectators. The appeal of Marcel Duchamp's formulation that "it's the spectators that make paintings" to the 1950s surrealists lay in its simply-worded yet radically suggestive elimination of the classical notion of art's intrinsic communicative faculty. Poetry and art came into existence through their encounter with an audience; reciprocally, the forms of intersubjectivity promoted by the existentialists were in turn mediated by the *non*-human objects and texts that provoked thought and interpretation by resisting immediate comprehension. By organizing the movement as a group who were as much witnesses at the "crossroads of philosophies," art objects, and values as they were participants in their coming-into-being, the surrealists subjected their individual thought, and the ideological presumptions they bore, to a constantly shifting dynamic. The surrealist experiment, then, might be understood as the attempt to mobilize art to "suppress the exploitation of man by man," by causing an insurrection *within* thought. This is a far cry from merely depicting insurrection or using wild, terrorist rhetoric to explain this political drive. Herein lies surrealism's essential contribution to twentieth century thought: not, as Jean Clair claimed, in "preparing the mind" for the atrocities of terrorism and the Holocaust, but in preparing the mind to defend itself against the forms of ideological closure that guarantee the continuation of such atrocities.

# PIERRE TAMINIAUX

# Breton and Trotsky: The Revolutionary Memory of Surrealism

The question that I raise in this essay is the following: Why have so many surrealists been, even temporarily, communist sympathizers? The historical ties between the surrealist movement and the political ideology stemming from the works of Marx and Lenin are undeniable. Nevertheless, it is quite striking to notice that, nowadays, there is no profound and radical rejection of the surrealist legacy based solely on political grounds. In contrast, one can say that much of the recent questioning of Sartre's preeminent position in the domain of twentieth-century French literature and thought has derived from the writer and philosopher's stubborn and inflexible attachment to the values and principles of Marxist politics. If one can often hear today a sentence such as: "Sartre got it wrong," one is less likely to hear a sentence such as: "Breton got it wrong," or even "Eluard got it wrong." How can one explain this difference of attitude toward surrealism and existentialism? In other terms, how can one still forgive or even forget the so-called "mistakes" made on one side and not those made on the other?

One could provide an easy and quick answer to these troubling questions: after all, surrealism never pretended to produce a true *littérature engagée,* in the Sartrean sense of the term. Indeed, one can argue that the political discourse of surrealism was often overshadowed by the aesthetic perspective on dreams and the unconscious that was put forward by Breton in the first *Manifesto.* In this sense, the surrealist revolution was above all of a poetic nature. One could always say that the surrealists were somewhat *dilettantes* in the field of politics, and that their dedication to this field was not that of true professional activists. In any case, it is quite clear that only a small amount of works produced by the surrealists could be characterized as political art. Landmark texts such as *Nadja* or *Le paysan de Paris* were not exercises in ideol-

**YFS 109,** *Surrealism and Its Others,* ed. Katharine Conley and Pierre Taminiaux, © 2006 by Yale University.

ogy but rather brilliant meditations on the magical and the supernatural power of everyday life. One could also refer in this regard to most
examples of automatic poetry, which were largely focused on the experiment with language according to a formalist approach. The most
notable exception was of course Aragon's highly polemical poem
"Front rouge." When the surrealists dealt more deeply with politics in
their creative endeavors, it was at a time when they had already distanced themselves from the rather authoritarian leadership of André
Breton. Desnos's vehement poems of resistance, for instance, such as
"Ce coeur qui haïssait la guerre" or "Le veilleur du Pont-au-Change"
were actually written during the Occupation, and thus, many years after his excommunication by Breton.[1]

One must inevitably go back first to the *Second Manifesto* of 1930[2]
in order to understand the complexity of the relationship between surrealism and Marxist ideology. This text was written in a climate of ex-
treme political tension and social turmoil. Breton proclaimed in it his
fundamental support of the basic principles of historical materialism.[3]
But he also demonstrated his profound hostility toward the leadership
of the French Communist Party and denounced all the intellectuals
who were betraying the spirit of surrealism by submitting entirely to
its authority in order to pursue their own personal ambitions. More
specifically, he accused them of being corrupt, morally feeble, and
essentially greedy. One of Breton's main targets was in this case the
controversial figure of Pierre Naville, who had been one of the early
companions of the movement and had played an active role in the publication of *La révolution surréaliste,* as he edited the first issue of the
journal with Benjamin Péret. For Breton, indeed, the unequivocal support of the proletarian revolution could never have led him to abandon
his artistic project in favor of an external political cause. Therefore, aesthetics had to prevail in its confusing relationship with politics.

In this perspective, Breton asserted his mistrust toward the idea of
a literature or an art capable of expressing the aspirations of the working class (*Manifestoes,* 155–57). Since the surrealists were all living in
pre-revolutionary times and since the revolution had not yet occurred
in their own country, that is France, the writer or the artist remained

1. These two poems appear in the collection *Choix de poèmes,* with an introduction
by Georges Hugnet, 99–100 and 103–109, respectively.
2. André Breton, *Manifestoes of Surrealism,* trans. Richard Seaver and Helen R. Lane
(Ann Arbor: The University of Michigan Press, 1969), 119–194.
3. See in particular Breton, *Manifestoes of Surrealism,* 142–43.

unable to translate the demands and the most profound desires of the workers. The surrealists were all coming from the ranks of the bourgeoisie and they all had to admit this undisputable truth. This was a matter of basic intellectual honesty. One could not legitimately support the idea of a proletarian culture within a world defined by the primarily economic interests of the ruling classes.

To enhance his argument, Breton referred here to the reflection of Leon Trotsky, as it appeared in *Révolution et culture,* a text published by Clarté on November 1, 1923. According to the Russian revolutionary leader's own words, there was still a long way to go before reaching the ideal state of a society free of all material constraints. The accomplishment of a true proletarian culture implied the existence of a social order in which most economic problems had already been overcome. In such a world, all children would have enough to eat and all men, liberated from their own natural selfishness, would strive for the knowledge, the transformation, and the betterment of the universe. Breton described Trotsky's remarks as admirable, and went on to severely criticize the clique of so-called proletarian writers and artists, who, under the dictatorship of Poincaré, pretended to faithfully represent the actual living conditions of the working class. These "fraudulent and wily characters," according to Breton's own terminology, could only agitate the ghost of Zola by taking advantage in an opportunistic manner of the suffering and the rage of the people. They were trapped in their own self-indulgence through the mere depiction of ugliness and sheer misery. It is obvious that Breton could not subscribe to this kind of naturalist approach: it was the opposite of what surrealist aesthetics was standing for. Any revolutionary perspective in the field of politics had thus to be translated in an artistic or literary project that was itself revolutionary. This meant an absolute trust in the power of dreams and human imagination and, therefore, the refusal to abide by the aesthetic rules imposed by a Stalinist French Communist Party.

In 1930, evidently, Western societies had been shaken by the stock-market crash of the previous year. Its devastating consequences could already be felt for millions of people worldwide who had either lost their jobs, seen most of their financial assets vanish, or experienced a dramatic decline in their standards of living. In this context, the preconditions for the rise of a proletarian culture set by Trotsky could not be met. When one usually talks about the historical background of surrealism, one either refers to the collective tragedy of World War I or to the surge of European Fascism in the 1930s. But surrealism also ap-

peared in the social and economic vacuum of the great crisis that followed the events of 1929. This vacuum made the need for a radical political change even more urgent, but it also enlightened the utopian
character of such a change. Moreover, the aesthetic dimension of revolution put forward by the surrealists ran the risk of being considered
secondary or even frivolous by all those who were fighting together for
this particular upheaval. As Breton wrote in this regard in the *Second
Manifesto,* the problem of social action was only one of the many manifestations of a more general problem, which was "the problem of human expression in all its forms" (*Manifestoes,* 151). The word: "expression" referred here primarily to language, and the first mission of
surrealism was thus to locate its own fight at the level of language.
Nonetheless, the conceptual tensions between the realm of aesthetics,
mainly that of poetry, and the realm of social or political reality had to
be resolved in one way or another. For Breton, undoubtedly, the historic
figure of Leon Trotsky offered the best opportunity for the synthesis of
these two essential issues.

The year 1930 was also marked by the start of a new surrealist publication, *Le surréalisme au service de la révolution,* which Breton directed from the beginning. The title of this journal asserted without any
ambiguity the surrealists' total commitment to the Third International, particularly in the event of an imperialist aggression against the
Soviet Union. The manifestation of unconditional solidarity with the
cause of the working class did not prevent Breton from affirming at
the same time the radical independence of his movement from any political authority, including that of the Communist Party, both in France
and in the Soviet Union. The most intriguing question stemming from
these conflicting statements thus became the following: How could
surrealism link its own destiny to that of international communism
while simultaneously refusing to embrace the dogmas dictated by its
political establishment in the name of its sacred artistic freedom?

In a series of 1952 radio interviews with André Parinaud, Breton
clearly expressed his relationship with communist ideology in the thir-
ties in human and personal terms.[4] He described the profound and lasting impression that the reading of Trotsky's book on Lenin had left on
him. This book acted as a sort of revelation, but this revelation was
more emotional than political. Consequently, Breton published an en-
thusiastic review of Trotsky's work on Lenin in the fifth issue of *La*

---

4. André Breton, *Entretiens* (Paris: Gallimard, 1969).

*révolution surréaliste*.[5] Breton claimed in the interview his dissatisfaction with the formulation of his own political ideas in this review. Nonetheless, he considered it to be his first major step in the direction of an authentic revolutionary consciousness and toward a profound understanding of both the principles and the ideals of the revolution. Breton confessed that his attachment to communist literature and thought was mostly sentimental: the poet always lacked the cold objectivity of the true ideologue. His involvement in the activities of the AEAR, the Association of Revolutionary Writers and Artists, which was presided by Paul Vaillant-Couturier, demonstrated again his relative marginalization within the community of Marxist intellectuals. Breton belonged there to the minority of members who represented left-wing opposition to the mainstream constituted by the hard-liners. This left-wing opposition to the Marxist orthodoxy of the time was clearly rallying behind the figure of Leon Trotsky.[6]

I would argue, therefore, that Breton, like Péret and other surrealists, was more of a Trotskyite than a true communist. But for him, the word: "Trotskyite" was shaped by a series of biographical events rather than by the abstract reality of ideas and systems of thought. In this regard, the cultural mission that was granted to him by the French Ministry of Foreign Affairs at the end of the 1930s played an essential role in his friendship with the former leader of the Russian Revolution. By being granted the opportunity to travel to Mexico through the action of the French government, Breton was able to realize two of his most important wishes: to go to a country which he always had dreamt of and to meet one of the men he admired the most. After a long period of wandering following his exile by Stalin, Trotsky had finally settled down in 1937 in Mexico where he had found a niche for his wife Natalia and himself thanks to the political support of then Mexican president Lazaro Cardenas, a liberal leader with socialist leanings.

This trip was not without potential danger, since the communist movement in Mexico was then largely infiltrated by Stalinists who were obviously suspicious of (if not entirely hostile to) the presence of Trotsky, the most vocal and popular opponent of Stalin, on their soil. Trotsky was already familiar with the ideas and actions of Breton in his favor and he wanted to express his gratitude to him. That is why he insisted on meeting the writer face-to-face. The painter Diego Rivera,

---

5. See Breton, *Entretiens,* 122–24.
6. For Breton's account of the activities of this association, see *Entretiens,* 170–71.

who had helped Trotsky to find political asylum in Mexico, arranged for this meeting between the two men. They rapidly became close friends during Breton's stay in the country. The two traveled through Mexico, and this common experience brought them even closer.

In one of his radio interviews with Parinaud, Breton stressed the profound humanity of the communist leader. It is this humanity that he considered to be the most remarkable feature of Trotsky's complex character.[7] In this sense, Breton's relation with Trotsky was above all personal. It did not come from the book, nor did it stem from a preconceived vision of the world imposed by revolutionary ideology. The obvious cultural and biographical differences between the two, between a Parisian bourgeois who also happened to be a poet and a Russian activist who also happened to be an intellectual, did not prevent them from finding a common ground in the domain of political affairs. Breton rapidly became fascinated by Trotsky's charismatic personality: according to Breton, this charisma was engendered by the power of an exceptional mind and by the outstanding intellectual capacities of a man who could always relate the world of ideas to that of everyday concerns. Their various encounters and discussions led to the publication of a joint text entitled "Pour un art révolutionnaire indépendant," which appeared in *Documents surréalistes*.[8] The purpose of this text was to define the particular conditions under which, from a revolutionary viewpoint, art and literature could participate in the collective struggle of the people for their freedom while remaining entirely independent of external pressures. This was the living proof that the two men had reached an agreement on the very identity of the artist and of his work within a society transformed by radical political changes.

Nonetheless, some noticeable differences remained between the two men. Breton acknowledged that the political activist who had been the main architect of the Red Army in revolutionary Russia was only marginally interested in artistic issues. In contrast, both Rivera and Breton represented a definite aesthetic sensitivity to which Trotsky was mostly alien. Trotsky, therefore, had been in many ways courted by the artistic community throughout the world, although he had actually demonstrated a relative ignorance of its needs and desires. This paradox underlined the general problems the surrealists had faced when dealing with the reality of communist politics toward art. Even

7. See Breton, *Entretiens*, 187–90.
8. Breton, *Conversations*, 150.

when they were interacting very personally with an enlightened leader such as Trotsky, a conceptual gap remained that could not be filled. In other words, the revolution always had to make a clear choice between its aesthetic and its strictly political definition: the Marxist approach necessarily implied the dependence of the artistic question upon the global economic conditions of its realization.

What inspired Breton in the figure of Trotsky was the promise of a new Soviet Union where Stalinism would be eventually overthrown. Evidently, for Breton, the rule of terror established by Stalin represented a profound betrayal of the original ideals of the Russian Revolution defined by both Lenin and Trotsky. The assassination of Trotsky by a Stalinist agent, on August 20, 1940, in his fortified house located in Coyoacan, one of the most affluent suburbs of Mexico City, was the fatal blow that forever separated Breton from the communist ideology of the Soviet Union.[9] In this particular case, Breton was forced to refer to the famous sentence by Lautréamont, "All the water in the sea would not suffice to wash away one intellectual bloodstain," and to take it literally and not just figuratively.[10] It is not just a historical leader who had been murdered in the most horrendous way, with an ice pick. It was also, and more deeply, any hope of reconciliation between the poet's conception of the revolutionary ideal and that of the political power.

One could easily accuse Breton of having tried to romanticize for many years the practical reality of the Revolution through his passionate praise for Trotsky. After all, no other artistic movement in modernity had used and exploited as much as surrealism had the word "revolution" for the sole purpose of expressing its own aesthetic project. In this regard, it is quite ironic that the same text that proclaimed the surrealists' unquestionable attachment to the values and principles of Marxism, that is Breton's *Second Manifesto*, actually began with the affirmation of the preeminence of rebellion and individual revolt in the general attitude of the surrealist artist toward a world dominated by bourgeois interests.[11] Revolution, in this sense, was too big of a con-

9. For a fictional but nonetheless faithful account of these dramatic events, see the film *The Assassination of Trotsky*, directed by Joseph Losey in 1972, starring Richard Burton as Trotsky and Alain Delon as his assassin.

10. Breton, *Conversations: The Autobiography of Surrealism, with André Parinaud and Others*, trans. Mark Polizzotti (New York: Paragon House, 1993), 150.

11. See Breton, *Entretiens*, 125–29. In these pages, Breton writes in particular that "the simplest surrealist act consists of dashing down into the street, pistol in hand, and firing blindly, as fast as you can pull the trigger, into the crowd."

cept for the surrealists, including Breton. They had abused its meaning too many times and did not really know what to do with the historical and political implications of the word. From the outset, "rebellion" or "revolt" better corresponded to the existential identity of surrealism. What truly mattered to Breton and most of his followers was more the powerful and urgent sense of a utopia that had to be shared by a vast community of artists and writers.

Trotsky himself had been a believer in the possibility of utopia, since he had dreamt of a classless society in which a profound and eternal harmony was going to reign between all men. In this regard, it is quite significant that our own post-historical era stemming from the universal rule of market economy and the collapse of the communist bloc has stirred a deep feeling of suspicion toward the very idea of Revolution. This widespread suspicion or even denial of the revolutionary project in today's world has not yet been able to spoil the word "utopia," however. It is as if this word had remained spotless, or even harmless. The utopian vision in general seems less frightening than the revolutionary one. It is both a more humane and a more flexible concept. This might be the reason why most surrealists (with the quite notable exception of Aragon) have until now escaped the kind of moral critique that Sartre has had to endure for their ongoing association with communist ideology. One can understand that surrealist politics had much more to do with the collective attempt to create an ideal world in which art and poetry would define the human condition as a whole than with the material and historical production of a state (and therefore of a political power) fostered by the dictatorship of the proletarian class. Etymologically, "utopia" is what is deprived of any proper place. The surrealists were searching precisely for an imaginary space that could only exist in the mind and the unconscious of the artist. In this sense, "utopia" is a revolution without the ideological and practical constraints of the Revolution. But maybe more importantly, utopia also constitutes a project of memory: while the Revolution, indeed, can pretend to get rid of the past and to proclaim the supremacy of the world to come, utopia necessarily rests upon the sense of a lost paradise to which mankind is destined to return. In this perspective, revolution is a utopia without a memory. It lacks the sheer sensitivity to the cultural legacy of the community. In contrast, this particular sensitivity had been key to Breton's reflection on the power of the magic and the supernatural for the poetic expression of man (which explains the presence of the word "memory" in the title of my essay). His subsequent praise of Charles Fourier's social philosophy ultimately demonstrated his relentless passion for the utopian discourse well beyond the strict framework of historical materialism.[12]

More than three decades after Breton's unequivocal support of Trotsky's politics, indeed, many participants in the May '68 movement, by choosing the late Russian leader as their ideological master, reiterated in their own phraseology this libertarian interpretation of his work and thought. In this sense, Breton's radical position had in some way anticipated the political ideals of the French youth born right after World War II. But what happened on August 20, 1940, in Mexico City also shattered, for a whole generation—and not just for Breton—the dream of a fusion between the revolutionary and the utopian project. In this regard, Trotsky's Mexican fortress,[13] in which he had been forced to live in order to protect his wife and himself from the constant threat of assassination, represented the ultimate and decisive contradiction of the "Glass House" conceived by Breton. The thick and high walls that surrounded it created instead a world of opacity, through which nothing could be seen. Metaphorically and symbolically, the Utopia of the Glass House was dying in this gloomy architectural—and political— reality. Transparency was no longer possible here: it had been made undesirable by some of the same people who had proclaimed beforehand the historical reason of a universal revolution.

The word "communism" appealed to Breton for a time no doubt because it entailed the notion of a community defined by its radical principles and values. The paramount concept of community, in his perspective, did not contradict the freedom of the subject in his poetic expression; it was able to resolve this particular tension between the individual and the collective. Bourgeois society emphasized the supremacy of individualism over any form of social solidarity. This individualism was driven by material concerns and made impossible the constitution of a true and lasting togetherness between human beings. Breton's perspective on community, therefore, did not deny the ethical

12. See, in this regard, Breton, *Ode à Charles Fourier*, ed. and intro. Jean Gaulmier (Paris: Librairie Klincksieck, 1961).

13. This house is now open to the general public. It has been turned into a museum that recreates in details the life of Trotsky and his wife during their stay there. One can therefore contemplate Trotsky's personal library, his desk, his typewriter as well as his last manuscript, a book on his deadly enemy Josef Stalin. One can also see a photograph that represents Trotsky surrounded by a group of Mexican friends, artists and communist supporters, and by Breton. Finally, one can read Trotsky's address book, which includes in particular the Parisian address of Benjamin Péret.

and artistic legitimacy of the individualist standpoint, but it required a profound questioning of its purpose within the framework of the capitalist world. In this sense, the community was meant to emphasize the spiritual and aesthetic identity of the individual in opposition to a social order that was stifling it. It definitely stemmed from Breton's hostility to the social atomization produced by modernity. Nonetheless, it did not ask for the integration of all members of society within its own structure. In other words, the surrealist community was never destined to become the whole of society, as opposed to its Marxist counterpart. In many ways, it operated and defined itself as a secret entity, with all its peculiar rituals and norms of behavior, and claimed its deliberate marginality as an existential necessity. If the tension between the individual and the community could be overcome, this was not the case for the tension between the community and society. The communist model, by contrast, ended up confusing the community with all members of the social order. There was no room for dissent or difference, since all men and women were forced to work toward the historical accomplishment of the revolutionary ideal. This community, therefore, was absolutist in its essential inclusiveness. It could not tolerate any expression of otherness, whereas the surrealist project underlined from the very beginning the need for an eccentric location of the artist and the poet. By "eccentric," I mean here both the sense of an original perspective and of a distant position toward the center of society. In order to belong to the surrealist community, one had to agree to a specific process of separation from the rest of mankind. The surrealist subject was not a universal one, as was the communist revolutionary. He recognized himself as other and did not pretend to reach the whole of humanity. A form of self-exclusion was at the source of his creative power and of his unique character. In this sense, to belong to the community did not mean to belong to the world but instead to a group that could always contradict it.[14]

Moreover, it is clear that surrealism could not be satisfied with a mere materialist interpretation of the world based on the supremacy of the economic predetermination of man. It implied a narrow identification of human existence with the sphere of labor and production. In *Nadja*, for instance, Breton expressed in the strongest terms his oppo-

14. For a philosophical discussion of the surrealist community beyond Marxism, see in particular "Le demain joueur," by Maurice Blanchot, in *L'entretien infini* (Paris: Gallimard, 1969), 597–619.

sition to the servitude of the working people trapped in a repetitive activity ("How I loathe the servitude people try to hold up to me as being so valuable").[15] His praise of wandering and daydreaming inevitably entailed the radical questioning of the significance of work for the human condition. He had to acknowledge the mere practical necessity of work for the basic survival of mankind, but he nonetheless refused to consider its moral value seriously and stressed instead the fundamental incompatibility between work and the revelation of life's meaning: "The event from which each of us is entitled to expect the revelation of his own life's meaning—that event which I may not yet have found, but on whose path I seek myself—*is not earned by work*" (*Nadja*, 60). Breton added in this regard that it was precisely this deep sense of the futility of work that his encounter with Nadja allowed him to grasp.

Surrealism could in no way embrace a global vision of the world for which work could be the main tool of man's emancipation, as in classical Marxism, beyond its obvious alienation within capitalist society. The famous (and infamous) sentence "work sets man free," that the Nazis borrowed from Marx and inscribed at the entrance of the death camps could never have been uttered by Breton and his followers. Its historical appropriation by the worst totalitarianism of the twentieth century proved surrealism, and above all its leading figure, to be right: work indeed constituted the ultimate negation of freedom, and its symbolic power would soon be manipulated by the most oppressive regimes in order to justify and enhance their own project of extermination. After all, the gulag was primarily defined by Stalinist propaganda as a mere labor camp where the prisoners were supposed to rediscover the "joys" and personal benefits of hard work and ongoing physical effort, according to a perverse and nihilistic form of Stakhanovism. In the context of French culture, the collaborationist regime of Vichy would in the same vein assert its own holy trinity, that of work, family, and homeland. Work, again, and particularly that of the peasant and the craftsman, was to be idealized in order to build an authoritarian political order based on tradition and social conformity. Communism, after all, started initially as a philosophical undertaking, in the shadow of Hegel and Marx. It was first a conceptual creation before being adapted, for better or worse, to the concrete domain of public affairs.

In other words, theory preceded historical events and political real-

15. Breton, *Nadja*, trans. Richard Howard (New York: Grove Press, 1960), 68.

ity, which was not exactly the case for Fascism, where the two were al-most simultaneous. Until the very end, indeed, theory could put some balm on all the wounds and the ills inflicted by the leaders who had used it for their own personal gains and ambitions. In particular, the in-tellectuals and the writers who remained communist sympathizers in spite of all the revelations concerning the numerous failures of the sys-tem could always brandish the texts from which it arose and stress their moral and spiritual greatness. Therefore, the concepts never really ceased to contain a philosophical and even existential truth. Commu-nism, in this sense, was engendered by the power of ideas and con-stantly relied upon this power to overcome its own evil. Its actual em-bodiment within social reality could thus be condoned and even forgiven as long as man was still aware of its origin (and of the very iden-tity of this origin). But for someone like Breton, this so-called moral su-periority of the concept did not make much sense, since surrealism was a way of life before being a worldview. In other words, the revolution in art and literature expressed itself above all in the personal experience of everyday life.

In the first pages of the *Second Manifesto*, Breton stigmatized "the baseness of Western thought" and emphasized the need "to take up arms against logic." He stressed the surrealists' fight against mere scholarly research and pure intellectual speculation and against all those who "used their minds as they would a savings bank" (*Mani-festoes*, 128–29). In the same text, he also put into perspective "the sov-ereignty of thought," by underlining the contradiction between the ab-solute character of human thought and its incarnation in numerous individuals of limited thought, while quoting Engels (*Manifestoes*, 154–55). In this sense, the poet could never be a real philosopher, nor could he be completely overwhelmed by the awesome power of ideol-ogy. The *Surrealist Manifesto*, thus, was not the *Communist Mani-festo*. Both evidently asserted the utmost urgency of radical change within modern Western society, but they differed in the sense that the concept, for Breton, opened up primarily to the issue of human expres-sion. By "expression," Breton obviously meant first and foremost the question of language. Communism established the essential relation-ship between theory and the realm of social action, whereas surrealism stressed the essential link between theory and the world of forms and symbols. It was thus to be expected that the two would clash sooner or later.

Moreover, the conflict that developed very quickly between Breton and the leadership of the French Communist Party demonstrated the profound contradiction between the spirit of surrealism and that of any political authority, regardless of its objectives and its program. In other words, by voicing his own personal grievances towards the Party, Breton highlighted the fact that surrealism could not abide by the rules of the institution. In this sense, it is not communism as such that he was opposing, but rather the institutionalization of the revolutionary political discourse. Breton had deliberately located surrealism outside of all literary, artistic, and academic institutions: there was no reason why the field of ideology would constitute an exception in this regard. The problematic nature of communism therefore stemmed from its willingness to rely on traditional power structures, which Breton abhorred. In this sense, revolutionary politics could never achieve the true intellectual independence and freedom of poetry. It is precisely this rather vehement rejection of the Party establishment that Breton projected on Trotsky: both men, indeed, had been confronting in their own country the repressive policies of the institution. The main difference was that Trotsky had experienced it from the inside, as a founding member of the Revolution, while Breton had always maintained a more distant if not ambiguous position toward all political power. Therefore, both men could share the same alienation from the communist elite and also the same feeling of betrayal by those who were supposed to be their friends and allies. The Trotsky that Breton met in Mexico was no longer one of the foremost leaders of the Soviet Union. He had become a pariah within his own movement, a figure of exclusion whose aura was essentially that of a victim of Stalinist madness.

Therefore, if the Revolution was not dead yet, it was precisely because such figures of dissent still existed and engaged in an ongoing personal dialogue in spite of the turmoil of history. Ideology could still be relevant as long as it was embodied in the world of human relations. Its potential humanity had to be strictly defined within these peculiar boundaries. If ideology, though, was overstepping such limits, it was doomed to become irrelevant.

In the *Second Manifesto*, Breton questioned the possible applications of Hegelian dialectics. He referred to "the colossal abortion of the Hegelian system," since the dialectic method was too often limited to its application in the field of social problems. Breton's allegiance to the principle of historical materialism, thus, was that of an "intuition of the world," according to Engels's formula, and not of a primitive or sectarian reduction of human existence to its purely material or socio-economic dimension. Philosophy had to be "outclassed," since the problems of love, dreams, madness, art, and religion could not solely be approached through the prism of theory. Instead, reality was primarily a matter of life and death and consequently an existential problem.[16] Historical materialism, in this sense, constituted a means and not an end in itself. It enabled the writer to build an image of his own liberation and of the original community to which he belonged. The words of poetry were also part of the material world and as such, they constituted the privileged elements of a radical transformation of the human condition. But the kind of materialism that Breton advocated differed from its purely Marxist version to the extent that it did not entail the supremacy of practical reason. In this regard, surrealism did not believe in the notion of a utilitarian language: art and literature were not to be celebrated because of their so-called usefulness for the social order, but rather because of their overwhelming unconscious power. This power was not the property of a particular class: it reflected instead the creative identity of man's inner life beyond his mere economic determination.

Communism attracted the early Breton because of both its antibourgeois (or anticapitalist) and its antifascist stance. The surrealists and the Russian revolutionaries shared the same foes and, therefore, they had to be allies. But the political engagement of the surrealist writer never truly reached the kind of critical intensity (the intensity of the relation to history) that one would find later in Sartre's work. It was driven more by emotions and feelings than by the rigor of philosophical discourse, as Breton's friendship with Trotsky shows unequivocally. Like most emotions and feelings, thus, it was destined to fade through the passing of time. Moreover, Breton never had real political ambitions, unlike other French writers of his generation such as Aragon or Malraux, who became closely involved either in the official structures of the Communist Party or in the executive branch of the Fifth Republic. Nor was Breton ever truly engaged in the French Resistance's movement against the Nazis either, as were fellow surrealist poets Desnos or Eluard. His American exile during the dark times of the Occupation signified instead, in many ways, the end of his radical political activities. If one single critical remark, therefore, can be addressed to the founder of the Surrealist movement on political matters, it is precisely that he decided to leave his country at a time when voices

16. See Breton, *Manifestoes of Surrealism*, 140–42.

of dissent were most needed in the face of evil. The very absence of politics, in this sense, constituted a political statement that lacked ethical legitimacy. In other words, silence and aloofness were not a convincing option in the midst of such collective oppression. Indeed, they were much more questionable than any endorsement of the Communist ideology in the 1920s or even the 1930s.

The aesthetics of surrealism definitely outlasted its politics. If the movement survived well after World War II, it was precisely because of its status as an avant-garde movement and not because of its revolutionary rhetoric. The avant-garde, indeed, was a literary or artistic concept, while the Revolution was primarily a political one. For Breton, the fascination for communism and the Marxist view of the world largely stemmed from the profound love of *elsewhere* (*ailleurs*), an essentially poetic notion that implied the sense of the unknown and of what could only be *imagined* because of its utmost remoteness. The Russian Revolution led by Trotsky had taken place far away from Paris, at the edge of Europe, and Trotsky's Mexican fortress was located even farther away, on another continent. For the surrealist poet, what could be imagined was always sweeter than what had to be lived. Communism was right, therefore, because it was first of all the stuff that dreams are made of. The "elsewhere" constituted a geographical other, but an other that could always be brought closer through the eternal power of words and visions.

# RICHARD STAMELMAN

# Photography: The Marvelous Precipitate of Desire

> This *trouvaille*, whether it be artistic, scientific, philosophic, or as useless as anything, is enough to undo the beauty of everything beside it. In it alone can we recognize the marvelous precipitate of desire. . . . Everything humans might want to know is written . . . in phosphorescent letters, in letters of *desire.*
>
> —André Breton, *Mad Love*

## THE CHIAROSCURO OF DESIRE

Among the sixty-four photographs the Hungarian artist and photographer Gyula Halász (who in 1932 would adopt the pseudonym "Brassaï," from the name of the Transylvanian town [Brassó] where he had been born in 1899) selected for inclusion in his album, *Paris de nuit* (1933), nearly one-half represent different states or acts of human desire. On the one hand, there are the desire for love and companionship, the pursuit of food, warmth, and shelter, and the search for pleasure and delight; on the other, the relief brought on by the removal of want, the physical satisfaction of human needs, and the comfort that sex, eating, and sleep provide, especially when sought and fulfilled in that ultimate site of desire, the city of Paris.

Beginning and ending with two double-page photographs of Paris's cobblestones, *Paris de nuit* leads the reader on a random tour along the chic boulevards and grimy backstreets, in front of the entrances of stylish hotels and less ostentatious *maisons de passe,* up the elegantly illuminated staircase of the Opera, on to the floors of popular dance halls, and through the city of light, here transformed by a surreal chiaroscuro into a city of shadows as well.[1] Along the way one meets Parisians at

---

1. Although Brassaï selected the photographs that compose *Paris de Nuit,* it was in probability his editors who determined their sequence in the book. Concerning the graphics and layout of *Paris de nuit* as well as the optics and poetics of photography it exhibits, see Marja Warehime, *Brassaï. Images of Culture and the Surrealist Observer* (Baton Rouge: Louisiana State UP., 1996), esp. 63, n. 48; Anne Wilkes Tucker, "Brassaï: Man of the World," in her *Brassaï: The Eye of Paris* (Houston: The Museum of Fine Arts, 1998),

YFS 109, *Surrealism and Its Others,* ed. Katharine Conley and Pierre Taminiaux, © 2006 by Yale University.

play—kissing on a park bench or hurrying in their limousines to *"les plaisirs de la nuit"* (no. 53); Parisians at work—bakers making the morning's bread, laborers polishing the tram rails, firemen extinguishing a blaze, print men adjusting immense rolls of paper, farmers bringing cauliflower and carrots to les Halles, flower girls, policemen, sewage cleaners, dancers, actresses, prostitutes; and finally, Parisians asleep: sheltered behind the facades of their apartments, or hidden in piles of straw laid out under the arches of buildings, or nodding off atop a pile of vegetables.[2] Above all, one is witness to Paris itself: its *grandes places* ablaze with lighted fountains and monuments (nos. 2, 8, 17, 48); its sleeping gardens crisscrossed by a mosaic of shadow and light evoking "a checkerboard of dreams" (no. 1); its densely outlined trees backlit by an off-camera street lamp (no. 9); its looming cathedrals cast in a blackness as soft as velvet (no. 7); and its coiling gutters awash in jet-black water (no. 14). From the rag picker on his knees foraging in dust bins (no. 61) to the man waiting at the door to enter a *"maison d'illusions"* innocuously named "chez Suzy" (no. 25); from the flower girl advising passersby to "Fleurissez-vous" (no. 33) to the host of tradespeople laboring to satisfy the city's hunger for news (no. 41), for bread, vegetables, and milk (nos. 36, 42, 62), for magazines, newspapers, and erotica (no. 45) and for spectacles (can-can dancers, circus performers, ballerinas, actors, and actresses) (nos. 20, 21, 22, 50, 51, 56, 59)—Paris presents itself as a theater of desire.

The banal, everyday life of the nocturnal city, so insignificant as to beg indifference, if not blindness, from all passersby except Brassaï— "Of what I see," he once wrote, "nothing passes by unnoticed, neither the stones, nor the people"[3]—takes on the gravity of enigma. This is a strangeness made all the more intense by the flatness of these "straight" photographs, which often reveal nothing more extraordinary than a man pausing in front of a Morris column to read an advertisement, or another man hurriedly buttoning his trousers as he steps away from a public urinal, or the shadows creeping up a prison wall (al-

---

35–36; Colin L. Westerbeck, Jr., "Night Light: Brassaï and Weegee," *Artforum* 14/4 (Dec. 1976): 34–40; and Rosalind Krauss, "Nightwalkers," *Art Journal* 41/1 (Spring 1981): 34–38.

2. Brassaï, *Paris de nuit* (Paris: Flammarion, 1987); *Paris By Night*, trans. Stuart Gilbert (Boston: Little, Brown, 2001). In a few instances, I have modified the English translations of the French captions; the photographs and their captions are indicated in my text by their numbers.

3. Brassaï, *Letters to My Parents*, trans. Peter Laki and Barna Kantor (Chicago: University of Chicago Press, 1997), x.

though behind it, as the caption notes, lurks the invisible guillotine). In Paris, at night, the gardens sleep quietly, the homeless sleep fitfully, night watchmen sleep warmly, and boats, tied to the quays of the Seine, move hardly an inch. Everywhere in these images there is the *darkness* of Paris: sometimes soft, velvety, grainy, palpable; sometimes hard, imposing, unyielding, compact, and dense like blocks of black. Everywhere in these images there is the *light* of Paris: sometimes misty, blurred, foggy, nebulous, rainsoaked, haloed; sometimes explosive, fiery, blazing, and flashing.

Always in Brassaï's photographs of nightbound Paris there is this coexistence—a collaboration, intersection, overlapping, entwining, contrast, symbiosis—of darkness *and* light, a simultaneity of opposites which, to the surrealist writer Louis Aragon, himself a nightwalker like Brassaï, constitutes one of the supreme experiences of surrealist experience: namely, the apparition of the marvelous (*le merveilleux*) in everyday life. The marvelous, Aragon wrote in *Le paysan de Paris*, published seven years before Brassaï's *Paris de nuit*, is "the eruption of contradiction within the real."[4] No such antithesis is more primeval than the explosion of light in darkness; for it represents the sudden apparition of the extraordinary within the confines of the familiar, the return of a collective repressed, the welling-up of ancient myths from the cellars of a modern metropolis, and the incarnation of the absolute, the sacred, the immemorial within the concrete banality of the here and now.

In *Le paysan de Paris*, Aragon offers a guided tour of a handful of forgotten *quartiers*, most notably the covered arcade known as "le passage de l'Opéra," a street whose hotels (catering to transients and prostitutes), cafés, restaurants, a hairdressing salon, a pharmacy, a theater, a haberdashery, and a bathhouse among other establishments invite the passerby into a spectacle of pleasure and a scene of desire, at once real and hallucinatory, realist and surrealist. "In everything base," Aragon writes, "there is some quality of the marvelous which puts me in the mood for pleasure" (PP, 37). Whether emanating from the phosphorescent, aquatic illumination of a shop window suddenly transformed into a mermaid's grotto, whether uncoiling serpent-like from the blond tresses, lit with "the electric pallor of storms" (PP, 40), of a woman in a *salon de coiffure*, light is "meaningful only in relation to darkness": "It is these mingled opposites which people our life, which make it pun-

4. Louis Aragon, *Paris Peasant* [*Le paysan de Paris*], trans. Simon Watson Taylor (Boston: Exact Change, 1994), 204; hereafter cited in the text as PP.

gent, intoxicating. We only exist in terms of this conflict, in the zone where black and white clash" (PP, 10).

This confrontation between black and white, a chiaroscuro of the marvelous, appears in nearly every photograph in Brassaï's *Paris de nuit*. How could urban night photography, which Brassaï was one of the first photographers to perfect, do otherwise since the blackness of night can leave no image without the presence of some source of light?[5] Among the many photographs in *Paris de nuit* in which the juxtaposition or clash of light and dark is indisputably evident, there is one that is particularly remarkable (no. 18). Under the narrow arc of a bridge a somewhat indistinct group of silhouetted *clochards* sits around a fire, "un feu de fortune," as the caption describes it. Its light barely illuminates the bridge's curved undersides. Thin, pencil-like reflections of light from the fire and from other unseen sources tremble on the darkened surface of the Seine. The upper stone abutment of the bridge, a massive block of black, stretches horizontally across the image, distancing the clochard's chthonic "cave" below—another world from time immemorial, primitive and mythic—from the "civilized" street that traverses the bridge above. This upper world is dazzlingly illuminated by a street lamp whose light is so powerful it seems, in a blast of haloed whiteness, to obliterate the glass fixture surrounding it. The leafless tree branches and the darkened façade of an apartment building, standing at some distance from the lamplight, are turned grey as the force of light, spreading wavelike from the lamppost, progressively loses its strength.

Yet, the *grisaille* of the upper street, by which the bridge's parapet, the windows of the apartment building, and the network of interlaced tree branches are clearly discernible, contrasts sharply with the massive blackness enveloping the world of misery and homelessness below. This is an irremediable, oppressive, unmitigated darkness, made all the more encompassing by the seven and a half inches of black running horizontally across the upper mid-section of the photo and the seven and a half inches of black running vertically down the left and right sides. In this literal and figurative underworld, the few points of light transform the cave of the bridge's arcing vault and its "mouth" into a transient home, making for a moment the *unheimlich heimlich*. There are two realms, here, each endowed with mythical and au-

5. See his "Techniques of Night Photography. Apropos of the Album *Paris de nuit*," in *Brassaï. From Surrealism to Art Informel* (Barcelona: Fundació Antoni Tàpies, 1993), 91–92.

tochthonous dimensions. Within the barely illuminated shelter of the bridge, a collective, primal past comes alive, as it did, albeit on a more personal level, for Marcel Proust, on whom Brassaï bestows the honorific title of "night photographer." Memory for Proust, observes Brassaï, was "a sort of night whose shadows swallow up our recollections, but out of which, sometimes, the images of the past loom when a sudden ray of light makes them emerge from the darkness."[6]

Into a modern city of light and delight, a primeval, prehistoric, uncivilized past surges into existence on the wings of piercing rays and diffuse haloes. It is a scene of desire in the form of want, need, and longing, the kind of desire that, unfortunately, deprivation keeps alive. Through the elemental struggle of light and darkness, which his knowing eye has captured, Brassaï represents the confrontation between want and desire, pain and pleasure, ignorance and revelation in keeping with a spirit at once *surrealist* (the discovery of the mythic, the uncanny, the grotesque, the bizarre within the commonplace), *socialist* (the portrait of the misery and dignity of the marginal inhabitants of the modern city), and finally *realist* (the unblinking representation of the nocturnal realities of work and play by which the city comes to live another day).

## SNAPSHOTS OF DESIRE

From two liquids mixed in a test tube a solid may suddenly fall to the bottom: a precipitate. Similarly, when surrealists came across a strange or fascinating object—the irregular white half-cylinder inscribed with bizarre graph lines and Italian words that Breton discovers in the Saint-Ouen flea-market in *Nadja,* or the strange wooden spoon, the underside of its handle resting on a miniature carved shoe, which he carts off from the same Parisian market in *L'amour fou*—something "drops out" of the situation, out of the chance encounter between an object and a subject, a thing and a self. This precipitate is desire itself, a desire that had remained unconscious, latent, invisible, inarticulate, and unformed until the forces of chance, awakening it from its state of dormancy, transform it into a haunting, disorienting experience of being. Photographs negotiate this identification or fusion of the I with what is other by recording their desire:

---

6. Brassaï, *Proust in the Power of Photography,* trans. Richard Howard (Chicago: University of Chicago Press, 2001), 106–7.

The countless pictures which . . . [the photographer] has stolen or extorted from time, are a living record. But they are more than that; they are moments of his own existence entered day by day in the pages of his log. They say not only: "Such or such a thing happened," but also "I was there," "I saw this thing," or even "*I was this thing.*" . . . It seems as . . . if man were never so entirely himself as when he forgets himself completely and merges his individuality with the sum total of things in the universe.[7]

In the "Transmutations," which Brassaï created in the mid-1930s—deformations of his photographic plates made by engraving surrealist-like forms onto their glass surfaces—Brassaï felt as if he were dredging hidden images and unconscious desires up to the surface of the glass plate: "As a sculptor, I have always limited myself to disengage a form glimpsed for an instant in a pebble collected on the sea-shore. In the same way, I compelled myself here to reveal the hidden figure which lay in each mental picture." As reality, manifest and latent, had been the point of departure for the photograph, so now the photograph, with its manifest and latent dimensions, becomes the point of departure for another creative transfer, once again provoked by unconscious desire and fantasy: "Almost as a sleep-walker, I witnessed these destructions and formations. The dislocated parts of the photographs reorganized themselves into new combinations." Photographs of nude women became the starting point for other images: "I cut their flesh as one carves a block to break loose the figure which it conceals."[8] And Brassaï's love of graffiti, which he began to photograph in 1933 and would continue to record almost to the end of his life (1984), reveals a similar fascination with the "released forms" of the primitive and the unconscious lodged in the material world of the everyday real.

The surfacing of transgressive desire from behind the walls of the banal present constitutes the "subversive energy," the "violent groundswell," the "mastering [of] the frenzy of the unconscious" that graffiti and photography record.[9] Such mythic and primitive apparitions are clearly suggested in *Paris de nuit*. For example, behind the wall of La Santé prison sits the guillotine, the embodiment of crime, punishment, and death (no. 12). Encircling the cemetery of Mont-

7. Brassaï, *Camera in Paris* (London: The Focal Press, 1949), 19.

8. Brassaï, "Transmutations," in *Brassaï. From Surrealism*, 201.

9. Brassaï, "From Cave Wall to Factory Wall," in *Brassaï. The Monograph*, ed. Alain Sayag and Annick Lionel-Marie (Boston: Little Brown, 2000), 292.

martre, isolating it from the carnal pleasures of Pigalle down the Boulevard de Clichy, or from the spirited revels descending the Montmartre hill, is the checkerboard pattern of a fence; its shadows (in this photographic *vanitas*) stand in sharp contrast to the harsh, eerie light that has momentarily abandoned these *quartiers* of earthly delights to take up residence on tombstones, crypts, and crosses alike (no. 31). Similarly, Egyptian antiquity and the divinities of ancient mythology arise in the place de la Concorde's fountain and obelisk (no. 17). In other words, the primitive mythic dramas of life and death, of creation and deterioration, of flux and eternity arise from the cobblestoned streets; time immemorial rends the fabric of familiar landmarks, highlighting the atavistic struggle for food, warmth, and light playing out beneath a Paris bridge. "The world of graffiti," writes Brassaï, "summarizes a whole lifetime in just a few major themes: birth, love, death. Birth, the image of man, spelled out, identified for the first time; the two sides of love, carnal and romantic; death, decomposing, nothingness, the great adventure."[10] Reality, thus, has its own unconscious, an as-yet unrevealed underside, a *sous-réalité* which translates into a *sur-réalité*. To present the real as it displays itself in its daily, fleeting ordinariness to the photographer intent on capturing it, is to seek whatever ghostly aspect of reality hides there "in a somnolent state, like a latent virus, just waiting until the breeding ground is right" for it to flare into being ("Parisian Grafitti," 169).

No wonder, then, that straight photography, when inspired by surrealist ideas, still remains attached to the everyday real. To photograph a crumpled bus ticket or a dab of hardened toothpaste, or a piece of used soap (as Brassaï did in his "Involuntary Sculptures") elevates realism to an intensity of magnification which "develops" (photographically speaking) its surrealist attributes.[11] "The possibility," Brassaï notes, "of penetrating the phenomenal world, of stealing its shapes . . . fascinates the photographer. Ah! This impersonal presence! This perpetual unknown! That most humble servant, the ultimate in dislocated being, lives only for these latent images. . . . He captures what is most positive, most solid, most real in them."[12] Like Goya and Daumier, the contemporary artist-chronicler-photographer aims to seize "the real-

10. Brassaï, "Parisian Graffiti," in *Brassaï. From Surrealism*, 170.

11. See Brassaï, "Involuntary Sculptures," *Minotaure*, 3–4 (1933), and Katharine Conley, "Modernist Primitivism in 1933: Brassaï's 'Involuntary Sculptures' in *Minotaure*," *Modernism / Modernity* 10/1 (2003): 127–40.

12. Brassaï, "Latent Images," in *Brassaï. From Surrealism*, 63.

ity of every day so intensely that he achieve[s] fantasy at one bound" (*Camera in Paris*, 13); and like Rembrandt, who is for Brassaï not only the first *modern* artist but the inventor of the snapshot *avant la lettre*, the photographer must note

> the things he sees, as soon as he sees them, before they change or he himself changes. . . . And because, in the excitement of seeing, every superfluous detail would be a waste of time, he is obliged not only to seize the impression quickly, but to reduce it to its bare essentials, extracting from it just that significant detail which indicates and suggests human beings and intimate objects. (*Camera in Paris*, 17–18)

Although the union of self and object, as occasioned by the chance precipitation of desire, is less narcissistic and egocentric in the case of Brassaï, known for his modesty and humility, than it was for his surrealist friends and collaborators—Brassaï refused to join the movement and was committed to keeping his artistic and political identity distant from any kind surrealist influence and interference—his conception of the photographic image is far from selfless, even though its reality depends to a greater degree on indirection and mediation.[13] One of his mantras was a sentence from Goethe that, even as it appears to tilt the balance in favor of the objective world, does not do so at the expense of the self: "'I have gradually been elevated to the height of objects,'" Goethe is purported to have written, words that Brassaï interprets as referring to the very "spirit of photography" by which the desires of the photographing self are made to coincide with the objects of its gaze.[14] If the photographic image is, as Brassaï defines it, "that irreplaceable witness of the instant and privileged substitute of reality" ("Transmu-

13. Brassaï was "a surrealist when he chooses," Werner Spies remarks in his "Brassaï: The Darkness and the Quarry" (*Brassaï. The Monograph*, 11). "'The surrealism of my pictures,'" Brassaï observed, "'was only reality made more eerie by my way of seeing. I never sought to express anything but reality itself, than which [sic] there is nothing more surreal'" (quoted in Sayag, "The Expression of Authenticity," *Brassaï. The Monograph*, 14). For a closer examination of the photographer's relationship with surrealism, see Warehime, 4–6, 37–44, 97–98; Ian Walker, *City Gorged With Dream: Surrealism and Documentary Photography in Interwar Paris* (Manchester: Manchester University Press, 2002), 144–57; Annick Lionel-Marie, "Letting the Eye be Light," in *Brassaï. The Monograph*, 160; Dawn Ades, "Photography and the Surrealist Text," in *L'amour fou. Photography and Surrealism*, ed. Rosalind Krauss and Jane Livingston (New York: Abbeville Press, 1985), 183–87; Manuel J. Borja-Villel, "Midway Between the Récit Poétique and the Expression of the Essential," in *Brassaï. From Surrealism*, 16–17; and Brassaï's own testimony in *Picasso and Company*, trans. Francis Price (Garden City, NY: Doubleday & Co., 1966), 15, 37–38.

14. Brassaï, "Words in the Air," in *Brassaï. From Surrealism*, 154.

tations," 201)—this because it is reality itself, namely, the things, people, gestures, bodies, forms, transferred through the medium of light to a photosensitive surface where they are re-embodied without interpretative intrusion or darkroom manipulation—then whatever this real may possess that is latent, subconscious, or phantasmatic will carry over, will adhere, to the photographic image. The ghosts of the real survive the transference; they are contained within the "depths" of the two-dimensional photograph. The visible is snapped along with the invisible; the breath of reality brings its "virus" into the air of the photo. And so when Aragon adopts the voice of a carnival barker and invites his reader in *Le paysan de Paris* to step right up and try the "vice," the "vertigo," of surrealism, he clearly wants the reader to learn that surrealism, this transgressive "offspring of frenzy and darkness," will open the doors to "les royaumes de l'instantané" (PP, 80): realms as instantaneous as snapshots.

## THE NOCTURNAL EYE OF DESIRE

Brassaï adored the night; in fact, he liked to say that he became a photographer (in 1929) primarily "to capture Paris by night." Night is a time in which otherness, formlessness, and an eerie sense of disorientation create a surrealist-like atmosphere of the bizarre, as Brassaï observed: "'Night unnerves us, and surprises us with its strangeness; it frees powers within us which were controlled by reason during the day. . . . I loved the way the night's apparitions hovered on the edges of the light.'"[15] As for the city of Paris at night, it is, according to Brassaï's *The Secret Paris of the 30's,* an album of texts and photos taken at the same time or soon after those in *Paris de nuit* (but not published until 1976), the Paris of another time and place, a city populated by the "other," for whom this realm "of pleasure, of love, vice, crime, drugs" was a necessarily "secret, suspicious world closed to the uninitiated":

> Drawn by the beauty of evil, the magic of the lower depths . . . I wanted to know what went on inside, behind the walls, behind the façades, in the wings: bars, dives, night clubs, one-night hotels, bordellos, opium dens. I was eager to penetrate this other world, this fringe world, the secret, sinister world of mobsters, outcasts, toughs, pimps, whores, addicts, inverts. Rightly or wrongly, I felt at the time that this underground world represented Paris at its least cosmopolitan, at its most

15. Lionel-Marie, "Letting the Eye be Light," 157.

alive, its most authentic, that in these colorful faces of its underworld there had been preserved, from age to age, almost without alteration, the folklore of its most remote past.[16]

So, the clochards who sleep on straw piles under the portico of the Bourse du Commerce are, as the captions in *Paris de nuit* explain, "modern descendants of medieval truands" (no. 26). The septaugenarian prostitute, La Môme Bijou, steps full-blown out of one of Baudelaire's "nightmarish" poems (no. 43). The narrow street, the passage de Clichy, with its five illuminated hotel signs and a pedestrian marker on which the block-letters of the word "interdit" are accentuated, is a site dedicated to "la Vénus des carrefours" (no. 27). No wonder that the police, as they cycle past a wall imprinted with the word "défense . . . ," their capes flapping behind them like wings, their whistles at the ready, seem more avian than human, a surrealist transmutation of species which their nickname "les hirondelles" (swallows) recalls (no. 28). Is it so surprising that a prostitute, plying her trade on the corner of la rue Quincampoix should suggest to Brassaï's imagination the fever for speculation created by John Law, director of finance under Louis XV, that played out at the same site in early eighteenth century Paris (no. 30)? The pimps, whores, criminals of this "other" Paris are, when all is said and done, no different from the *genii loci* who once haunted the same neighborhoods during the time of François Villon.

Surrealist imagination is present as well in the transformations Brassaï's eye perceives in the flora and fauna of this strange, nether urban world. Not only is the "ageless" Môme Bijou, bedecked in a dozen rings and endless strands of pearls wrapped around her neck, wrists, and fingers, a "fantastic apparition that had sprung up out of the night" surprising the photographer as a "rare and monstrously beautiful insect" would strike an entomologist (*Secret Paris of the 30's*); she is also an epiphany unto herself, the apparition of the Sphinx *en plein Paris*. The outdoor urinals of Paris are more than toilets. As shelters for homosexual encounters they are reincarnations of Sodom and Gomorrah, made modern by the addition of illuminated billboards advertising such *apéritifs* as Byrrh. Their ugly vulgarity undergoes a striking metamorphosis, an aesthetic mythification, turning them into "strange and delicate monuments" (no. 11). But the archaic world of ancient mythology surges forth most strikingly in Brassaï's photograph of the cesspool

16. Brassaï, *The Secret Paris of the 30's*, trans. Richard Miller (London: Thames & Hudson, 1976), np.

cleaners, moving from tenement to tenement to remove the sewage captured in basement holding tanks (no. 29). Smoke arises from the boilers of their horse-drawn pumps, hoses coil and curve like snakes, dark figures bend and kneel, and the street fills with a hellish light and, one would imagine, smell.

Despite the emphasis on night in its title, *Paris de nuit* presents few sites or landscapes that are not transformed, not made *other*, by the intervention of light. Lighting, Brassaï once told an interviewer, is "'to the photographer what style is to the writer.'"[17] The shadows cast by the fence of the Luxembourg garden trace a dream mosaic onto the "empty alleys" of the night-enclosed *jardin* (no. 1). Not surprisingly, the Arc de Triomphe, the Place de la Concorde and the Tour Eiffel are adorned in a "fabulous sumptuousness," so "splendidly lit" that the Place de la Concorde resembles a dining table set with an exquisitely delicate silver centerpiece (nos. 2, 17, 48, 57). The Paris sky is "luminous" (no. 4); the poster for Mistinguett, the *chansonnière*, announces to *le tout Paris* that she is appearing in a review called, appropriately enough, "*Paris qui brille*" (no. 10). The irregularly lit windows of an apartment building propose to the spectator's imagination a host of "living enigmas" (no. 13). Sparks from tramway tracks under repair create a "ravishing fireworks display" (no. 37) much more powerful than the "red glow" bathing the face of a man asleep beside a fiery brazier (no. 39). The bare back of a baker, seen through a basement window from above, is "bathed in light" (no. 42), as are the naked torsos of actresses on stage, their bodies caressed by the "pencil-thin shafts of spotlights" as photographed from a catwalk above (no. 50). Even nature itself is electrified; blossoms stand at attention as they fan out like "extraordinary candelabras" from chestnut trees (no. 54).

## THE SUNFLOWER OF DESIRE

If the "marvelous precipitate" that falls out of solution when chance brings one person into the orbit of another is desire itself, the kind of desire that Brassaï in *Paris du nuit* is concerned with photographing, then there is no better example of the prophetic, incantatory nature of this desire than Breton's poem "Tournesol," an automatic poem (in reality, a kind of undeveloped "photograph") Breton wrote in May or June 1923 and quickly forgot, but which takes on great significance in his

17. Sayag, "The Expression of Authenticity," 16.

life when, on the night of May 29, 1934, he meets an extraordinary woman and in her enchanting company walks for hours from Montmartre to the Latin quarter. Not only will this woman, Jacqueline Lamba, become his second wife almost three months later, but the events of their nocturnal promenade, it will occur to Breton soon after their encounter, were prefigured almost to the letter in the lyrical verses describing Paris at night which the "Tournesol" poem of eleven years earlier had evoked. Interesting as well is the second meaning of "tournesol"; in addition to signifying the movement, the "turn," of a flower toward a life-giving source of light, "tournesol" (litmus paper) alludes to a chemical change, or turn, in color. Breton, as the poem's premonitory image predicts, will turn in the direction of a light about to dawn in the world of his affections, a light in the form of a woman who will change, not only the trajectory, but the coloration, as it were, of his life. The surrealist "chemistry" of desire, when set in motion by the operations of chance, produces definite reactions: precipitates, on the one hand, and chemical signs (red or blue) of metamorphosis, on the other.

To describe his burning desire to seize the truth of the real world, to capture the intensity of its elusive and wordless presence, Eugenio Montale, the Italian Nobel laureate, once commanded, in a poem dedicated to the sunflower, "Bring me the plant that leads the way / to where blond transparencies / rise, and life as essence turns to haze; / bring me the sunflower crazed with light."[18] For Breton, the iconic sunflower of his automatic poem is crazed not by the light of a midday sun but by that of a Paris night; heliotropically, he turns toward this nocturnal light, that of the city and that of his newly found love, the way Brassaï is phototropically drawn to the chiaroscuro of the *grands boulevards* and the narrow *passages* of the city of light. The photographer strolls through Paris taking shot after shot, continually aware of the intersections of light and shadow, a light (an earthlight, a *clair de terre*, as Breton once called it), whose chalky spots and blurred rings (the effect of halation) could, absent Brassaï's careful manipulation, ruin the equilibrium between dark and light he so wished to capture. Crazed, even "maddened," by his new beloved, Breton interprets her

18. Eugenio Montale, *Collected Poems 1920–1954*, rev. ed., trans. Jonathan Galassi (New York: Farrar, Straus and Giroux, 2000), 47. For the relationship between desire, light, and painting, a "calligraphy of desire," see my "'La courbe sans fin du désir.' *Les Constellations* de Joan Miró et André Breton," *Cahiers de l'Herne* 72 (1998): 313–27.

apparition in terms of the surrealist chiaroscuro of night and light: "It was as if suddenly, the deepest night of human existence were to be penetrated . . . all things being rendered totally transparent, linked by a chain of glass without one link missing. . . . It may be the beginning of a contact, unimaginably dazzling, between man and the world of things."[19]

When first seen in a Montmartre café where Breton is meeting with friends, Jacqueline dazzles the poet with, among other things, her coloration; she is "swathed in mist—clothed in fire." Her color takes "on a deeper hue from her face to her hands." Her head appears haloed by "the extraordinary pale sun of her hair like a bouquet of honeysuckle"; she is "*scandalously* beautiful"; strangely, she moves "in broad daylight, within the gleam of a lamp" (ML, 41). She leaves the café, and outside as early evening descends she gives Breton a rendezvous for later. At midnight they meet again and talk for two hours before leaving the café at 2. An hour later they find themselves in les Halles, a favorite haunt of Brassaï, as evidenced not only in *Paris de nuit* (nos. 35, 36), but in one of the three photographs he gave Breton to illustrate the "Nuit de tournesol" essay. Reaching the sunflower-like Tour Saint-Jacques (illustrated by yet another Brassaï photograph) and then moving on to the Hotel de Ville, the poet begins to feel physically overwhelmed and excited by the city: "I succumb to the wonderful dizziness these places inspire in me, places where everything I have best known began" (ML, 47). His prose turns rhapsodic: "Let this curtain of shadows be lifted and let me be led fearlessly toward the light! Turn, oh sun, and you, oh great night, banish from my heart everything that is not faith in my new star" (ML, 49). At the flower market, the next site in the couple's amorous trajectory, Breton describes with a meticulous realism, reminiscent of Brassaï's illuminated sacks, carts, and vegetables waiting to be unloaded at les Halles, the spectacle of dormant flowers "still numb from the night" lying on the pavement "in pairs as far as the eye can see" (ML, 49). Here, on the Quai aux Fleurs, the poet acknowledges the flowering, as it were, of his desire: "A clear fountain where my desire to take a new being along with me is reflected and comes to slake its thirst, the desire for that which has not yet been possible" (ML, 49). But the possible has become real; the flowering of the city, of the night, and

19. André Breton, *Mad Love* [*L'amour fou*], trans. Mary Ann Caws (Lincoln: U Nebraska P, 1987), 40, hereafter referred to as ML. The passages quoted in the epigraph are also from this translation (13; 15).

of hope coincide with the halo of light enveloping the beloved object of desire: "You are so blond, so attractive in the morning dawn, that it understates the case to say that you cannot be separated from this radiant expansion" (ML, 51). This blossoming of feminine light in harmony with the expansion of the poet's desire and this encounter of the exterior world with the interior self are confirmed by the union of the poet's pulse with that of the city, for "the heart of Paris beat[s] throughout the stroll . . . in unison with mine" (ML, 64).

Breton becomes his own reader, when in *L'amour fou* he undertakes a line-by-line interpretation of the sunflower poem, showing how an allusion or association here and a metaphor or an image there refer literally to the events of what he calls in a typically surrealist oxymoron, "the *night* of the sunflower." Interestingly, the "photographic" images that the poem's lines offer in intermittent waves of sensation and flashes of perception (an effect of the poem's automatist and paratactic style) call to mind Brassaï's snapshots, his "instantanés." Each line of the poem is like a little picture, caught on the fly, immobilized for a second, before another image takes its place. Moving rapidly from cafés to bridges and streets, from statues to chestnut trees and les Halles ("a farm . . . in the heart of Paris"), a young woman traveler, walking on tiptoes, carries in her handbag the "dream" of the narrator-poet at the very moment it seemed despair was darkening the sky of his existence:

> The Innocents' Ball was in full swing
> Chinese lanterns caught fire slowly among the chestnut trees
> The lady with no shadow knelt on the Pont-au-Change
> Rue Gît-le-Coeur the stamps were no longer the same
> . . . . . . . . . . . . . . . . . . . . . . . . . . . . . .
> I am the pawn of no sensual power
> And yet the cricket singing in the ashen hair
> One evening near the statue of Etienne Marcel
> Gave me a knowing look
> André Breton it said go on. (ML, 55–56)

With the encouraging chirp of the cricket removing all doubt from the poet's mind, Breton's life turns in a new direction, except that the reality of this new life will have to remain dormant, and its image undeveloped, for eleven more years. The chance meeting with a woman in a crowded café will finally serve as the catalyst, as the "developer," that will make manifest what has remained latent, transforming the imaginary into reality, as Brassaï perceptively observes of Proust:

To Proust's question: "But what is a memory we no longer can recall?" . . . this other question corresponds: "But what is a photograph
that has never been developed?" No memory, and no latent image, can
be delivered from this purgatory without the intervention of that deus
ex machina which is the "developer," as the word itself indicates. For
Proust, this will habitually be a present resemblance which will resus-
citate a memory, as a chemical substance brings to life a latent image.
The role of the developer is identical in both cases: to bring an impression from a virtual to a real state. (*Proust*, 139)

From the forgotten negative, out of the discarded poem, and from
the silence of the subconscious, a precipitate is born: the precipitate of
desire, recorded in the light and shadow of the photograph, in the dark,
poetic letters inscribed on paper, and, according to Breton, in "the white
curve on black ground we call thought" ("Tournesol," ML, 55). The in-
dexicality of the photo—the fact that it points to the incontestable
presence of what it represents, the way, for example, the imprint of a
leaf in snow testifies to the reality of the once present leaf—also helps
to explain how a photograph is a precipitate, a virtual image, projected
into visibility through a series of chemical reactions set in motion
when light and object meet. It is, as Rosalind Krauss has shown, "a kind
of deposit of the real," what Brassaï discovered in his transmutations
to be the "debris [that] gives to our obsessions, to our dreams the flash
of the instant, the breath of reality."[20] In Brassaï's case, his love for
Paris—he was fascinated by "the way Paris lives and moves and how
one moves with it"—is translated into the angles, lighting, reflections,
shadows, sites, and subjects of his photographs. The eros of the city,
which his photographs raise from the shadows of virtuality, is less a creation of his art than a discovery of his eye. This is a gaze that voraciously
consumes the city in order to reveal what has persistently been present
but that we have failed to see: namely, the Paris that holds "me captive
to the last blood cells and nerve fibers of my being" (*Letters to My Parents*, 110).

20. Rosalind Krauss, "Photography in the Service of Surrealism," in *L'amour fou.
Photography and Surrealism*, 31 and Brassaï, "Transmutations," 201.

# ROBERT HARVEY

# Where's Duchamp?—Out Queering the Field

It's a facile pun for French speakers to draw "field" out of "Duchamp," since "du champ" means "of the field" or even "out of the field": the pun is nevertheless a serviceable twist for signifying the close link between the work of art that Marcel Duchamp made of himself and the profound transformations that occurred, during his lifetime and since, in the rules of the game played on the field known as the "art world." Those transformations—a veritable revolution like the one the surrealists dreamed of fomenting—required that Duchamp remain staunchly independent of all schools, movements, and formations. Being outside, in itself, was not particularly queer; but the effect that Duchamp had on the field was resolutely queer. Some still maintain that everything in the wake of Duchamp is art, and that therefore nothing is. I will maintain that instead of a tabula rasa, this explosion of possibility for the art—object or otherwise—should be seen as an irregular, unpredictable, delightfully complex terrain. Duchamp didn't clear the field, he queered it.

Grasping what surrealism was—which entails tracing the movements that it impelled and the transformations it accomplished—proves to be accurate (and certainly more interesting) when one ranges over the terrain where Marcel Duchamp willingly allowed his identity to float free of all constraints. This identity anarchy deforms, reforms, and informs the work of art as well as Duchamp's relation to work per se. The result is a recomplexified topography for art in general—a queered field.

"Action" is undoubtedly too strong a term to describe the inflection of seemingly anything that came in contact with Marcel Duchamp—unless one subjects the term "action" to a thoroughgoing critique. For example, if one can accept the counter-intuitive notion that something

YFS 109, *Surrealism and Its Others,* ed. Katharine Conley and Pierre Taminiaux, © 2006 by Yale University.

like "action" can be produced by a person at complete rest, then Duchamp can be considered to have strived to act. To prove to himself and to whomever might care that painters might not be as stupid as the old French adage, "*bête comme un peintre*" [stupid as a painter] asserts, we know that he quickly developed the technique of creating art with his brain instead of brawn conducted through the brush. What aesthetics has retained from Duchamp's passage through its field is that ideas not only make art: they *are* art, sometimes. We might also consider, for a moment, where "action," considered in all of its possible degrees, is situated within the dialectic of labor and leisure. Alternating with or, apparently sometimes in tandem with periods of febrile and fastidious activity, Duchamp engaged in concerted laziness. These variants of—or deviant manifestations of—"action" deserve the attention of more than a few moments. And I suggest that they bring us near the heart of what attracted Breton to Duchamp and what, at the same time, guaranteed the preservation of Duchamp's autonomy from surrealism.

"Everybody loved him," Gertrude Stein once wrote.[1] How true! Accounts are unanimous in testifying—first and second-hand—that women and men alike were mad about Marcel. At the very least he didn't displease. His mild manner, his wit, his politeness—even when he occasionally expressed disagreement, concern, or stubborn opinion—all worked to incline affections toward him. Women queer and straight desired him with unbound intensity. No doubt lots of men did too. You adore me, you love me: everyone adores Marcel, but often doesn't get loved back. Although I think it's a little outré to assert, as Amelia Jones has, that Duchamp "served as a desired object for many of the artists now termed New York Dadaists,"[2] who could ever attribute anywhere near as much adoration to the likes of André Breton? By all accounts surrealism's animator was insufferably self-centered, dictatorial, hopelessly misogynistic, and homophobic.

The premise of this volume is to examine surrealism in light of *that which is not surrealist.* How then, specifically, does Marcel Duchamp—as other—contribute to the shaping of surrealism? I'll begin, as my prologue suggests, by positing that Duchampian *otherness*

1. Gertrude Stein, *The Autobiography of Alice B. Toklas* (New York, Vintage Books, 1990), 133.

2. Amelia Jones, "'Woman' in Dada: Elsa, Rrose, and Charlie," in Naomi Sawelson-Gorse, ed., *Women in Dada: Essays on Sex, Gender, and Identity* (Cambridge: MIT Press, 1998), 153.

begins in the sheer endearing qualities of the man. This lovability enabled him quite singularly to implement a one-man program to disrupt the stodginess of the art institution. Duchamp's knack for intriguing everyone—including, especially, Breton—is in large part a product of a curiously *active* form of *laziness* (a paradox that will have to be unraveled as we go). Duchamp opened a variety of avenues along which this active laziness manifested itself; I will later focus on one well-known one (Rrose Sélavy) and suggest the tracings of a new one. Whereas surrealism, prematurely announcing the revolution, ultimately played into capitalism's propensity to commodify everything, Duchamp parodied the commodification of art and thus never succumbed to the trappings incurred after ideological breakdown.

In this essay, in other words, I will attempt to adumbrate some vectors in the force field of Duchamp's queerness that extend well beyond sexual practices and politics into the realms of aesthetics and, ultimately, ethics. This should enable the reader to see clearly that irreconcilable differences lay between programmatic and worldly surrealism on the one hand and the type and scope of the epistemology that Duchamp's investigations and creations organize on the other.

"All painting and sculpture exhibitions nauseate me," Duchamp wrote to Jacques Doucet in 1925, "and I would like to avoid being associated with them."[3] This expression of position is typical, unwavering, and applies to all exhibitions—even those, including surrealism shows, to whose organization he contributed; even those later devoted to his own work: "I beg you to avoid all exhibitions and events about me," he admonished Henri-Pierre Roché in 1952 (N° 210). His aversion to the dynamics and destructiveness of group activity is such a commonplace corroborated, moreover, by abundant evidence that it's superfluous to rehearse. This fact alone would probably suffice for succinct dictionary work to explain why he abhorred "isms" and was never a Dadaist nor became a card-carrying surrealist. However, before we get into the Duchamp-surrealism dialectic, let me stress that their irreconcilability did not at all preclude collaboration and a certain level of

---

3. All quotes from Duchamp's letters are found in Francis M. Naumann and Hector Obalk, eds., *Affectionately, Marcel: The Selected Correspondence of Marcel Duchamp* (Ghent and Amsterdam: Ludion Press, 2000). Translations from the French are sometimes modified by me; Duchamp's letters in English are of course left as he wrote them. Addressee's name, date of letter, and number attributed to it in the above edition will be noted in parentheses in all subsequent occurrences. This letter is dated 19 October 1925 and is N° 85 in *Affectionately, Marcel.*

friendship—even with the ofttimes insufferable André Breton. It would be dead wrong, in other words, to blithely infer or proclaim that Duchamp had nothing to do with surrealism or, a fortiori, with André Breton.

Garbo and Marcel: kindred spirits in the desire to be left alone. "I am managing to live more or less the same way as in Paris," he writes to Man Ray from New York, "no telephone, no cocktail parties—a bit like a badger, but it's the only way to solve the social problem" (23 July 1944, N° 154). Conveying to Brancusi his approval of Francis Picabia's new attitude toward society in 1925: "He's far less militant than before and seems contented with sunshine and the easy life. That's the best way to really tell idiots to fuck off" (N° 86). "The more I live among artists, the more I am convinced that they are fakes from the minute they get successful in the smallest way. . . . Don't bother naming a few exceptions to justify some milder opinion about the whole 'Art game'" (to Katherine Dreier, 5 November 1928, N° 100). His faithful sponsor would soon suggest that Waldemar George write a book on Duchamp. The reaction came swiftly and with uncharacteristic elaboration: "My attitude about the book is based upon my attitude toward 'Art' since 1918. . . . It can be no more question of my life as an artist's life: I gave it up ten years ago; this period is long enough to prove that my intention to remain outside of any art manifestation is permanent. . . . The third question is that I want to be alone as much as possible. This abrupt way to speak of my 'hardening process' is not meant to be mean, but is the result of a '42 years of age.' Summing up, [p]lease understand, I am trying for a minimum of action, gradually" (11 September 1929, N° 101). Marcel must have the pettiness of cliques in mind when he expresses his exasperation to Pierre de Massot ("from my *pissotière* I spy Pierre de Massot") that "the bullshit of Paris is boundless" (30 August 1933, N° 106).

Out of this epistolary thicket, a pattern to accompany dogged independence appears: a desire for inertia that materializes in the readymade while identitary promiscuity will provide the decoy.

## FELLOW TRAVELLER

Isms and schisms, cliques and klatches were not Duchamp's cup of coffee. He'd go out drinking with a few independent spirits in New York, but the only club he ever joined was for chess—arguably the foremost of his passions. And he only tolerated chess players because with them you didn't have to bare your soul. "Nothing as usual. Chess as much as possible: at least chess players don't *talk*" (to Suzanne Duchamp, 8 January 1948, N° 175). Alone, then, yet perhaps against all odds, Duchamp writes, as late as 1944, that "Breton is the only one I see regularly" (to Roché, N° 159).

Aloof and slick: this was Duchamp's (non-)stance vis-à-vis his peers, even before the notoriety gained by the *succès de scandale* of *Nude Descending a Staircase, N° 2* at New York's Armory Show in 1913. So later, when Breton identified Duchamp as a living precursor of surrealism, his persistent elusiveness only served to augment the hero-worship Breton lavished on him. As early as 1922, Breton wrote to Jacques Doucet that Duchamp was "the man from whom I would be the most inclined to expect something, if he wasn't so distant and deep down so desperate."[4] Typical case of transference, for it was Breton who was desperate to delve programmatically into Duchamp's putative unconscious as he did with everyone in the surrealist inner circle. But as comments he made in the 1950s, disapproving of Michel Carrouges' study of "bachelor machines" amply indicate, Duchamp gave little credence to the theory of the unconscious. Consequently, Marcel Duchamp's (or, rather Rrose Sélavy's) many salacious puns, which to Breton were the most remarkable poetic phenomenon in years,[5] were to Duchamp expressions of fully conscious cognition.

If there was one study on his work that got him really worked up, it was Michel Carrouges' *Bachelor Machines*, first published with the Arcanes psychoanalytic publishing house in 1954. And in perfectly antipsychoanalytic terms, he made perfectly clear to Breton what got his dander up and just how Carrouges missed the whole point (which was laughter): "Using the Green Box, Carrouges has brought to light the underlying process with the meticulousness of a sub-mental dissection. No need to add that his findings, even if they form a coherent whole, were never *conscious* when I was working out my strategy because my subconscious is *mute* like all subconsciousnesses and that my strategy had more to do with the *conscious* need to introduce some '*hilarity*' or at least some humor into such a 'serious' subject." Duchamp's underlining, twice, of the word "conscious" speaks voluminously of his conviction (that jibes with that of Gertrude Stein, moreover) that there is

4. Letter dated 12 August 1922, quoted in Calvin Tomkins, *Marcel Duchamp: A Biography* (New York: Henry Holt and Co., 1996).
5. Cf. *Littérature*, December 1922.

only consciousness—no unconscious. And his dismissal of Carrouges and his book, *Les machines célibataires*, could not be more definitive: "For me, there is something other than *yes, no,* and *indifferent*—it's the absence of investigations of this sort, for example" (to Breton, 4 October 1954, N° 235).

Nor did he have any particular political convictions. Such apathy would have disqualified him for the kind of fellow-traveling with the surrealists that linked Sartre, for a while, to the Communist Party. Yet he was not at all confrontational in his differend with surrealism, like his close friend Francis Picabia was, and he provided steady—if episodic—accompaniment to André Breton's endeavors right up to the latter's death in 1966. Indeed, the homosocial dimension of their collaborative friendship did not escape Duchamp: it was "a man-to-man friendship," he explained to Georges Charbonnier in 1961, "one could even see in it a homosexual element, if we were indeed homosexuals. We were not, but it is all the same. Our friendship could have turned into a homosexual one if it had not expressed itself in surrealism instead."

An unwavering heterosexual, or so he says, Duchamp was not absolutely indifferent to the object choices people make, but he was conceptually and performatively experimental in the domain, and went out of his way to defend the role of homosexuals in society. Rrose Sélavy is the most obviously sustained experiment in gender trouble. His œuvre—from *Fountain* to *Étant donnés*—is a tautology (or "patatautology") of conceptual experimentation. As for his defense of homosexuality, we have only to consider Duchamp's response to Frank Lloyd Wright's boorish question posed to him at the Western Round Table on Modern Art in 1949 when he'd just said that he did not consider homosexuality to be degenerate: *Wright*—"You would say that this movement which we call modern art and painting has been greatly in debt to homosexualism [*sic*]?" *Duchamp*—"I admit it, but not in your terms. I believe that the homosexual public has shown more interest or curiosity for modern art than the heterosexual public."[6] I would ask the reader to simply place this in the scales opposite Breton's homophobia as expressed in the infamous "Research on Sexuality." Queneau must necessarily be a "pederast," according to "Dédé," be-

6. Douglas MacAgy, ed., "The Western Round Table on Modern Art" in Robert Motherwell and Ad Reinhardt, eds., *Modern Artists in America* (New York: Wittenborn Schulz, 1951), 30.

cause he finds the "sentimental ideas of pederasts" altogether acceptable; Breton imperiously puts an end to discussion of a subject so abject to him that he cannot even name it.[7]

Radically independent, Duchamp could never join the surrealists. Apolitical and queer (straight or otherwise) *avant la lettre,* and Breton's awe of him notwithstanding, he was radically disqualified for surrealism. Yet Duchamp and Breton maintained a certain degree of friendship and, most importantly in this context, Duchamp lent his services to numerous surrealist endeavors virtually to the end of his life. In addition to allowing various works of his to be included in surrealist exhibits as well as providing puns and artwork for publications, Duchamp was the invisible but principal hand behind the design of several famous exhibits. There was the major "Exposition Internationale du Surréalisme" of 1938 organized at the Galerie des Beaux-Arts for which Duchamp created the ceiling environment consisting of over a thousand loosely stuffed coal bags. Then there was the "First Papers of Surrealism" show on Madison Avenue in 1942 where the space among paintings was obstructed by miles of string that Duchamp had strung haphazardly. To add to the confusion, Duchamp incited Sidney Janis's children to run through the maze as they wished while people were trying to look. If they were challenged by an adult, he'd instructed them to answer politely that Mr. Duchamp had given them permission to do so. Trying to revive surrealism after the war, Breton got Duchamp's help with "Le Surréalisme en 1947" which showed in both Paris and New York. They collaborated on the mise-en-scène, but the most significant Duchamp contribution was the limited edition catalog with its *"prière de toucher"* cover.

All this good will and good humor offered to Breton culminates in the sour note hit after Duchamp good-naturedly helps out once again. But this time the incorrigibly imperious, jealous, sectarian Breton wraps his faithful friend on the knuckles. The "Surrealist Intrusion in the Enchanter's Domain" ran at New York's D'Arcy Galleries from late 1960 to early 1961. Breton, in Paris, put Duchamp in charge of selections for the exhibit. Salvador Dali's work appealed as much to Duchamp's mind as to his eye, and Duchamp continued to appreciate it even after Breton had banished Dali from the surrealist group. Apparently Duchamp thought that Breton had mellowed. But he was wrong again. Breton blew his stack in a letter of protest. Not bother-

7. *La révolution surréaliste* 11, 15 (March 1928), 38.

ing to defend his decision, Duchamp satisfied himself with a simple expression of vexation: "Dear André, Allow me not to prevaricate in the form of 'explanations and excuses.' I simply regret, now, having agreed to organize this exhibition" (11 December 1960, N° 265). After nearly forty years of collaboration on a variety of surrealist endeavors, even with his faithful friend Marcel Duchamp, André Breton had not changed.

## PUTTERING

Surrealism advocated the unleashing of the (putative) unconscious to engender an artistic vocabulary capable of extending the reach of art from that field's delineation as handed to high modernism by nineteenth-century aesthetics. But the field for experimentation that surrealism purported to broaden proved resistant to their methods of expansion. The spurts of curatorial activity that I have just described were exceptions in Marcel Duchamp's checkered career. Most of the time he had other fish to fry.

As if afflicted with ADD, Duchamp tried his hand at every painterly manner available—impressionism, symbolism, fauvism, cubism— and, then, starting with the readymade, began *effacing* the boundaries tacitly imposed on the theoretical questions art could legitimately raise. Abetting this febrile impatience, Duchamp embodied affable passivity, a woefully deficient disregard for the virility tacitly required of vanguard artists. Like futurism (and Paul Claudel's remark in *Le Figaro* that it was essentially pederastic notwithstanding), surrealism was heterosexist through and through. Duchamp's practice, on quite another hand, settled in discreet puttering at the pole opposite avant-garde dynamism. Hovering in the vicinity of inertia, cultivating a pondered laziness, Duchamp, however, expanded the field of aesthetics beyond surrealism's stunted program. In this regard, the title of the second edition of Pierre Cabanne's famous book of Duchamp interviews— *L'ingénieur du temps perdu*—is not only extremely clever, it is revelatory: Duchamp was an engineer both *in* his spare time but, most intriguingly and improbably, an engineer *of* spare time.[8]

Duchamp might have been reading Paul Lafargue's tract, *Le droit à la paresse*, or, more likely, Eugène Marsan's playful *Éloge de la paresse*. In any case, he appreciated recognizing his own work ethic in the book

8. Pierre Cabane, *L'ingénieur du temps perdu* (Paris: Belfond, 1967, 1977).

Man Ray gave him shortly before the former's death.[9] "Lazy" is how he systematically characterizes himself in his letters. The tone might sound like a lament, but he was quite as content to cultivate sloth as he was to allow dust to collect. Way back in 1913, having just received news about the Armory Show in New York City and the splash that *Nude Descending a Staircase, N° 2* made there, Duchamp began a letter from Neuilly to his friend, the connoisseur Walter Pach, in this way: "I have been wanting to write to you for a long time but am so lazy that I don't even attempt to make excuses any more" (2 July 1913, N° 3).

A Duchamp who putters is a Duchamp in tatters. He disperses what energy he has into a multiplicity of odd jobs and dead ends; dissipation is his middle name. Nowhere near surrealist focus and determination. "In tatters" was the pictural treatment he adopted in painting his sisters. *Duchamp du signe* and *Marchand du sel* consist almost exclusively of fragmentary writing. His missives are telegraphic. "I'm writing to more or less everybody at the moment. Bores me to tears. It's a pity cables are so expensive: they're so convenient" (to Suzanne, 17 October 1916, N° 13). (How he would have liked e-mail!) He dreams of dictionaries and makes compendia as often as single works: *Tu m'*, boxes green and white, and so on. Rrose Sélavy's puns are disparate despite their consistent salaciousness. And Duchamp's silence ("my only attitude is silence" [N° 117]), as overrated as Joseph Beuys endeavored to claim it was, punches holes in the claims of consistency and consolidation of discourse. He retreated enigmatically, retracting like a hermit crab from social and communal action. Once in his retreat, once in his burrow, however, only then did he focus like a fuss budget.

What Duchamp tirelessly calls his laziness feeds, most probably, on boredom. And plenty of things bored him—even his own protracted work on the *Large Glass*. Already, in a letter to Crotti in 1918, he had referred to it as that "big piece of trash" [*cette grande saloperie*] (8 July 1918, N° 19); four years later, he was complaining to Man Ray about what a drag it still was on his existence (April or May 1922, N° 46). But in the interim, he claims (perhaps a bit too much in an effort to impress

9. "I really like the praise of sloth [*l'éloge à la paresse*]!" (to Man Ray, 9 August 1967, N° 281). The note in Naumann and Obalk's edition of Duchamp's correspondence (op. cit.) identifies the book as Lafargue's *Le droit à la paresse*, 1880 (*The Right To Be Lazy*, NY: Gordon Press, 1973). I would contend that it might well be, as Duchamp's exact words indicate, Eugène Marsan's, *Éloge de la paresse* (Paris: Hachette, 1926).

Ettie Stettheimer, whom he wooed in vain): "Since I don't lift a finger, I want you to work. Dada Logic" (6 July 1921, N° 40).

As executed by Duchamp, work and idleness are often barely distinguishable. "I have been very lazy lately," he reports to Dreier, "that is to say concentrating on the sale of my box which by the way is almost a success" (15 December 1934, N° 117). That to Duchamp's thinking active laziness parallels a similarly curious noncontradiction at a global scale finds no better expression than in this remark to Roché on 21 August 1945: "there really is sincere relief at the thought of peace and heightened by the titillating threat of the atomic bomb" (to Roché, 21 August 1945, N° 162). In 1927 Monte Carlo, perfecting his system to win at roulette, he writes to Picabia that the activity "is deliciously monotonous. Not a trace of emotion. As you can see, I haven't quit being a painter: Fortune is now the topic of my drawings" (17 April 1924, N° 75). He thanks Ettie a year later for buying into "my scheme. I sent you a bond, registered delivery yesterday, which is the only one of value among the ones you have seen because it's stamped. If you have another one keep it as a *work of art* but the 20% will be paid to you on the one I'm sending you with this letter" (27 March 1925, N° 83; MD's emphasis). Arguably, much Duchampian idleness *is* work that creates surplus value out of nothing!

It is truly ironic, given the associations we inevitably make between what Duchamp abhors most about the artistic world and surrealism, that it is to Breton that he explains with the most precision just what the dialectic of activity and idleness is, for him: "It's no longer months now but years that have gone by since I last gave you any sign of life. Clearly you know more or less everything about me as I remain constant in my outward inaction [*inaction externe*], which unfortunately is accompanied by a tendency toward spiritual stultification due to the current mediocre bullshit firmly established as something for the public good" (to Elisa and André Breton, 25 December 1949, N° 185).

## EVERYWHERE A READYMADE

Proof that the field of art, for us, has been blown wide open and definitively queered comes when we recognize that we are in a world dominated by the readymade. The argument with examples will not be made here. Suffice it to say that by displaying and illustrating Duchamp's recognition (while bringing us to recognize it) of this revolution that he fostered within his lifetime, we fill in a fuller picture of surrealism. Michel Van Peene and Dominique Chateau have begun the project of a catalogue raisonné of readymades.[10] But already, one can see—and I'm sure they can see—that this project is destined to remain "definitively unfinished." In sketching a typology of readymades, Duchamp and Arturo Schwartz were already suggesting that even origins *of* and destinations *for* this new way of viewing objects could continue to multiply like a virus not dissimilar from William S. Burroughs' concept of the word virus.[11]

The vision of a world littered with readymades is previewed in 1913. As the first note in the "White Box" tells us, Duchamp was wondering if works-that-are-not-of-art could be made.[12] The affirmative answer is the sinuous line one may draw from the bicycle wheel all the way to the sculptural waste product sculpture so reminiscent in form of Brancusi's *Princess X,* baptized *Objet dard,* and that Ron Padgett slyly translates as "'ard Object." Duchamp's telegraphic epistolary style reaches new heights in a 31 January 1954 letter to his sister Suzanne and brother-in-law Jean Crotti. In one line he announced the deaths in close succession of Louise and Walter Arensberg; on the next, "I've been married since 16 January to Teeny Matisse. No children yet, except for the 3 ready made." Teeny, née Alexina Sattler in 1906, had three children by Pierre Matisse—Paul, Pierre-Noël and Jacqueline—all born in the 1930s. It was fairly safe to assume that she, now 48, and Marcel, now 66, would have no offspring of their own. But hey! Who needs kids when you've got readymades?

The gamut of Duchamp's readymades contributes to Duchamp's ethic of laziness and their use/uselessness tie in with the queerness. The dust accumulation left patterned by the components of the *Large Glass* is intricately of or by the artist, yet absolutely gratuitous: all Duchamp had to do was wait. Dust is the physical world's correlate of what humanity offers with sloth. In agreeing with Man Ray to memorialize this field of dust by a photograph, Duchamp brings the readymade beyond itself, into a realm where the positive photo is of a nega-

10. "Petit catalogue raisonné des ready-mades," *Étant donné—Marcel Duchamp* 1 (1999): 132–45.

11. "Listes des readymades de Marcel Duchamp," in *La raie alitée d'effets. Apropos of Marcel Duchamp,* ed. André Gervais (Montreal: Hurtebise HMH), 1984.

12. Michel Sanouillet and Elmer Peterson, eds., *Salt Seller: The Writings of Marcel Duchamp* (New York: Oxford University Press, 1973), 74.

tive (the dust) of a positive (the bride and bachelors) that is essentially negative because transparent (the glass).

Loafing produces readymades. The solution to man's enslavement to labor is being resolved. A true revolution. "I'm hardly doing any work at all" (to Louise Arensberg, 24 August 1917, N° 17); "I'm not working at anything" (Katherine Dreier, 25 May, 1927, N° 93); "You win: you've written to me while I am still in a state of bewilderment and idleness" (to Man Ray, early Fall 1942, N° 145). All true enough when one thinks that doing nothing and making readymades is almost the same thing. It's not the ampoule that's important, it's the 50mm$^2$ of Paris air that counts. Or doing nothing more "productive" than thinking about "a transformer designed to utilize slight, wasted energies such as: the growth of a head of hair, the fall of urine and excrement, laughter, forbidding glances, sighs" (*Salt Seller*, 191–92). This is what Duchamp will call harnessing the energy of the infra-slim: "when the tobacco smoke also smells of the mouth which exhales it, the two odors are married by infra-slim" (*Salt Seller*, 194). As another example, Denis de Rougemont went on record quoting Duchamp in 1968 as having said that "the sound or the music which corduroy trousers, like these, make when one moves, is pertinent to infra-slim."

One must waste one's time carefully, precisely, and with economy when putting waste to wasteful "uses." Criticism too may become a readymade whose authorship is different from that of the artist by a mere infra-slim margin. In Jean Suquet's book on the *Large Glass*, Duchamp recognized a readymade of his own work that perfectly reverses the economy of ownership: "I would really enjoy reading your 'my mirror'" (9 August 1949, N° 181). Here, we see a variant on the R. Mutt attribution for *Fountain*. Reading Duchamp's instructions to Roché for replacing the *Paris Air* that Walter Arensberg had broken is a paradigmatic opportunity for measuring the fussiness that an engineer of spare time must maintain in order to queer the field of art: "Could you go to the pharmacy at the corner of Rue Blomet and Rue de Vaugirard (if it's still there—that's where I bought the first ampoule) and buy an ampoule like this: 125cc and the same measurements as the sketch [to scale, inserted]. Ask the pharmacist to empty it of its contents and seal the glass with a blow torch. Then wrap it up and send it to me here. If not Rue Blomet, somewhere else—but, as far as possible, the same shape and size. Thanks" (9 May 1949, N° 178). Even vacuous verbosity, when well arranged, becomes readymade words in a can: recounting to Jacques and Gabrielle Villon the 1949 Western Round Table on Modern Art, where he contested Frank Lloyd Wright's homophobia, he wrote: "You can imagine what gibberish [*bafouillage*], but no matter. The conference proceedings will come out in October when corrections have been made and the nonsense [*âneries*] spoken tidied up (15 June 1949, N° 180).

### RRAMBLING RROSE

> I never kept sheep
> But it's as if I'd done so.
>
> —Alberto Caeiro

A rose is not always exactly a rose is not always exactly a rose. A rose bush is different from a climber is different from a rambler. A bush is best trimmed and contained; a climber is best trained on a two-dimensional surface *en espalier;* but the quality that a rambling rose delivers to the amateur is its prolific and erratic ranging over that thirty-foot cherry tree without, for all that, killing it.

Rrose Sélavy may have been born in 1920[13] and she may have lived a long flourishing life twinned to Marcel, but she was not his only other. To Roché s/he was always Totor (short for Victor), Brancusi and Morice shared the same name (only they could tell the difference, one supposes); s/he was Marcélavy, Marcel Duchit, Martini, Marcel Duche, Duduche, Marcellus, Pierre Delaire, Ducreux and a dozen others, according to indices in various publications. "In 1923," however, as Thierry de Duve astutely points out, "the list opened itself to infinity with the ready-made aliases chosen in *Wanted.*"[14] In the text below the mug shot on the wanted poster, the person whose arrest will be rewarded is "George W. Welch [not Bush, but almost], alias Bull, alias Pickens, etcetry, etcetry." All perfectly queer.

With utmost seriousness, Marcel shares his assessments of Rrose Sélavy with those he knows will be interested. "She's something of a *femme savante* which is not unpleasant" (to Jacques Doucet, 26 October 1923, N° 68). On the practical side, there's even something of the readymade payee for bank accounts in Rrose: twice—in 1933 and 1934—Roché received requests for checks to be deposited in her name.

---

13. Cf. letter to Henry McBride, July? 1922, N° 51.

14. Thierry de Duve, "Echoes of the Readymade: Critique of Pure Modernism" in Martha Buskirk and Mignon Nixon, eds., *The Duchamp Effect: Essays, Interviews, Round Table* (Cambridge: MIT Press, 1996), 107.

Besides being a bit of a blue stocking, she must have been good at laundering money for her alter ego, Marcel (Nᵒˢ 104 and 113). "I see everybody," he once wrote with tantalizing contradiction to Yvonne Chastel, one of the many women for whose attentions he longed and who reciprocated with adoration, "but in reality, am close to nobody. It's one of the advantages of my being a pimp [mac]. People have a lot more respect for me than before. Their attitude gives me a big laugh" (15 July 1922?, Nᵒ 53). The whores over whom Duchamp lorded it were of course his own selves promiscuously dwelling in paintings, puns, readymades—pawns in his game joyfully played alone on a field now forever queered.

I'd be more than willing to believe (and the cohort of Duchamp scholars who believe similarly is growing) that although Marcel never had sex the way a heterosexual Marcelle would, it was as if he had. For, as feminist and queer theorists have amply and convincingly argued, to have been penetrated so—even in the mode of some Kantian "as if"— is to know something of the forces of oppression in the world the way queers and women do. This should be just as clear to anyone as the fact that Alberto Caeiro is every bit as much Fernando Pessoa as Rrose Sélavy is Marcel Duchamp. Alberto and Rrose were not only heteronyms enabling the subjects who carried them to make their art, write their poetry, grind their chocolate: they were fully conscious and navigable ontic givens that enabled ethics based on aesthetics.

Letting identities ramble free and flourish may have begun with Rrose, but it was much more than a simple "game between I and me." Duchamp incarnated the death of the author and thrived on it. Nothing to do with Thanatos, here. For in Marcel's resistance to all norms, Rrose Sélavy is not a defeatist shrug of the shoulder, she is a paean to life. Marcel, you're leading me on (*tu m'aguiches*), Rrose rumbles. You feminize and eroticize me in making me you (*tu m'es*), Marcelle moans. You engender me while taking precaution not to knock me up (*m'engrosser*). In fact, this queer couple has mastered the art and science of sexless engendering one of the other.

### QUEER

The retorsions that Duchamp was bent on bringing to bear upon the field of artistic creation did not await his (re)birth as Rrose Sélavy. As queer as it might have seemed to some for Duchamp to sign *Fountain* as R. Mutt, this wasn't convoluted enough for Marcel. Delighted with himself for the antic, he writes to his sister Suzanne that: "A *female friend of mine,* using *a male pseudonym,* Richard Mutt, submitted a porcelain urinal [*pissotière*] as sculpture. No reason to refuse it: there was nothing indecent about it. The committee decided to refuse to exhibit this thing. I handed in my resignation and that juicy piece of gossip will have a certain value in New York. I felt like organizing a special exhibition for things *refused* at the *Independents,* but that would be a pleonasm!" (11 April 1917, N° 15). As the terms I've underscored in this epistolary excerpt may indicate, Duchamp delighted in twisting gender-defined identity to the point that this criterion for identity might dissipate in a pleonastic cloud. As I have endeavored to show, here, Duchamp's work is intrinsically queer—not so much on the side of product as on the side of process.

While the queer purport of Duchamp's work was not (necessarily) fueled by his own sexuality, Paul B. Franklin has convincingly demonstrated its foundations in intimate solidarity with (and knowledge of) queer culture in Paris and New York in the early decades of the twentieth century.[15] In light of Duchamp's position as one of surrealism's others, I would like to supplement Franklin's admirably exhaustive findings with a couple of remarks. We know that over the course of 1922 and 1923, Robert Desnos wrote out some 199 puns, claiming that Rrose Sélavy had telepathically dictated them to him.[16] When Rrose read them, she wasn't overly impressed[17]—either by their quality or by the claim that they came to Desnos through a process not unlike the workings of the unconscious: a psychic level to whose existence he gave little credence. She was nevertheless sufficiently amused to make the queer suggestion that she and Desnos become engaged (Tomkins, 248).

Assuming, as we must, that Breton got wind of Rrose's proposal to surrealist soldier Desnos, it's difficult—recalling the former's imperious (and defensive) censorship of all discussion of homosexuality in the surrealists' so-called "research on sexuality"—to imagine the "pope" much amused. There's plenty of evidence to support the hypothesis

15. Paul B. Franklin, "Object Choice: Marcel Duchamp's *Fountain* and the Art of Queer Art History," *Oxford Art Journal* 23/1 (2000): 23–50.
16. First published in *Littérature* N° 7 (December 1922), these puns were reprinted in *Corps et biens* (Paris: Gallimard, 1930).
17. "I forgot to tell Jean [Crotti] in my last letter that I'd replied to Breton about the puns in 'Desnos asleep.' Some were really very good but, in most of them, the rhymes were too apparent and sounded much more like Desnos than me" (to Jacques and Gabrielle Villon, 25 December 1922, N° 61).

that, had the unlikely occurred and Duchamp *had* become a member of the surrealist group, he would certainly have had to break with them over the sexuality flap. After all, many who *did* actually join the group cut short their association following the episode: to name two, Queneau quit and Crevel killed himself. Taking their sexism and queerbashing the further step and rendering them programmatic or axiomatic was just the type of aberrant result of group dynamics that Duchamp avoided by giving the surrealists a wide berth.

The closest contemporary parallels to "Duchamp's masquerade as a woman" that Amelia Jones has identified are "the Baroness Elsa von Freytag-Loringhoven's bizarre, sexually ambiguous self-performances in the streets of New York [and] Charles Demuth's images of non-heterosexualized male desire" (143). Although, as I hope I have successfully suggested, Rrose Sélavy is only the most obvious manifestation of a queerness that cannot be reduced, as Jones seems to do here, to identity performance, I agree wholly that these figures, who were unrecoverable by schools, seriously challenged what those very schools dreamt of challenging. One can no more claim that a lone wastrel—no matter how active—could complexify the terrain of art than that General or Emperor (or even President) so-and-so could single-handedly change the course of human history: both signifying formations are metaphors and, as such, assume mythical power concentrated at the disposal of a unitary alleged human subject. Empirical realization of these tasks is in the empire of networks, thousands of plateaus. The most one can assert with certainty about art (and the world of events) is that the field(s) was (or were) already skewed in the first place. This is tantamount to saying that queerness has everything to do with the nature of the field occupied by the agents we are and that queerness has little, if anything, to do with our putative subjecthood. Duchamp's œuvre stands as proof that the best way to reveal the truly unpredictable complexity of art is not to play the field, as his friends the surrealists endeavored to do, but to let the field play you, me, "us."

RAPHAËLLE MOINE

# From Surrealist Cinema to Surrealism in Cinema: Does a Surrealist Genre Exist in Film?

It might seem strange, even iconoclastic, to call upon the notion of genre in order to understand surrealist cinema. As one already knows, surrealism manifests itself above all in a group, which is characterized by its restless destiny. In this sense, surrealist films are strictly works created by one or more members of the group. Indeed, surrealism is not about a genre, but about an aesthetic movement, based on founding and program-like texts (the *Manifestos*). It is also about revolutionary and subversive ideas involving artistic creation as a way of life, and one's relationship with the world, with oneself, with others, and ultimately with society. Moreover, since the constitution and the recognition of a cinematographic genre involve a large number of works that share thematic, formal, and stylistic traits, the notion of genre implies a principle of both repetition and quantity. Recognition of a "generic formula" is thus contingent on a minimum of longevity and stability in artistic production.[1] Conversely, aesthetic schools and movements, particularly avant-garde and modernist ones like surrealism, often set themselves apart by an ephemeral quality that prohibits all large-scale artistic production that would accomplish their principles. After an often evanescent period of growth and blossoming, these movements exercise a widespread underground influence that has nothing in common with the fundamentally repetitive serial model, although susceptible to variations, that is being proposed by generic formulas. Finally, schools and movements spring up in art history in order to oppose dom-

---

1. For definitions of genre in formulaic, narrative, and cultural terms, see, for example, John Cawelti, *Adventures, Mystery and Romance: Formula Stories as Art and Popular Culture* (Chicago: Chicago University Press, 1976); Thomas Schatz, *Hollywood Genres: Formula, Filmmaking and the Studio System* (New York, Random House, 1981).

**YFS 109,** *Surrealism and Its Others,* ed. Katharine Conley and Pierre Taminiaux, © 2006 by Yale University.

inant ideas and to impose an aesthetic, a style, and a new gaze, while genres embody or set a tradition. This refusal of the norm and this strategy of rupture have never been so clearly displayed as in the radical ideas of surrealism.

The purpose of this essay is not to make surrealist cinema a genre. Instead, I will show in the first part of my essay that, even if the notion of genre comes across in many ways in surrealist works, it is impossible for surrealist film (in the strictest sense) to constitute a genre. However, today it appears that the term "surrealist film" is used frequently, not only to designate an exclusively surrealist production (*La coquille et le clergyman, Un chien andalou,* and *L'âge d'or*), but also to characterize an entire variety of films directly or indirectly influenced by surrealism, or *read and interpreted* as such, sometimes without any established affiliation. Thus there has been a *genrification* of surrealism in cinema: the term "surrealist film" has become a category of interpretation. As such, it is comparable, if not to a generic category in the fullest sense, at least to a *generic operator.* I will return to this notion in the second part of my essay: it indeed resembles the recent conceptions of genre as a mediating tool between works and their public. Consequently, I will show how "surrealist film" has been able to become a true generic operator in the field of French criticism.

## GENRE(S) AND SURREALISM

The "mauvais genre" that one commonly equates with genre films certainly contradicts the aesthetic value judgment on surrealist films, but it is still accepted, even openly, by the surrealists. When used for cinema, the term "genre" almost systematically refers to "genre films," that is to commercial productions deprived of all ambition and artistic intention, while the notion of the literary genre does not necessarily evoke genre literature (popular literature or paraliterature), but instead categories, either theoretical or historical, that are completely literary (the essay, the novel, the epic, and so on). The contemporary use is inclined to circumscribe the cinematographic genre within popular culture and the mass production of familiar stories, with familiar characters in familiar situations, all with a familiar cinematographic treatment. Bearing this in mind, the evocation of genre in the case of surrealist film can seem iconoclastic, even more than simply incorrect. It seems iconoclastic because of the aesthetic value attributed by critical tradition to surrealist films (*Un chien andalou* or *L'âge d'or* are part of the pantheon of cinematographic works). But it is less incorrect than it seems if one considers that, in the specific case of the surrealists, the line between art and non-art is blurred. The famous definition of surrealism by André Breton clearly shows this: "a psychic automatism in its pure state, by which one proposes to express—verbally, by means of the written word, or in any other manner—the actual functioning of thought. Dictated by thought, in the absence of any control exercised by reason, exempt from any aesthetic or moral concern."[2] In other words, before any capacity of the cinematographic image to express the "actual functioning of thought," it is the cultural illegitimacy of young cinema that pushes the surrealists, not without a certain dandyism, to hang out frequently in neighborhood places, to look for "disorientation" and "magnetic" moments in series like *Les mystères de New York* and early Charlot and Picratt series,[3] and to appreciate "American comedies with easy sentimentality, or violent films where one sees lost people who rehabilitate themselves and fall into the arms of the ideal woman after having had the most miserable of lives."[4] As Alain and Odette Virmaux write, "by systematically seeking out the worst commercial production, one didn't only aim at offending people of culture and good taste, but also the zealots of the 'seventh art,' the fans of aesthetic cinema, the first cinephiles."[5] It is therefore genre cinema that interests the "surrealists" when they themselves are the spectators.

When one considers the surrealists' creative involvement in the cinematographic universe, one is forced to recognize that it is outside of cinema and actually in literature that one can undoubtedly find a true genre created and developed by the surrealists: the screenplays, written independently of all plans and desires of filming and sometimes even declared to be "unfilmable,"[6] where cinema functions as nothing more than a point of reference, for example, editing and typography that evoke "real" screenplays. These were published in many reviews during the mid-1920s or in separate editions, and this primarily literary

2. André Breton, *Manifestoes of Surrealism*, trans. Richard Seaver and Helen R. Lane (Ann Arbor: The University of Michigan Press, 1969), 26.

3. Breton, "Comme dans un bois," in *L'âge du cinéma* 4–5, special surrealist edition (August–November 1951), 26–30, reedited by Alain and Odette Virmaux as *Les surréalistes et le cinéma* (Paris: Éditions Seghers, 1976), 277–82.

4. Michel Leiris, *L'âge d'homme* (Paris: Gallimard, 1939), 224. (Translations here and throughout are the translator's, except as otherwise noted.)

5. Virmaux, *Les surréalistes et le cinéma*, 14.

6. This is the case in *Trois Scénarii* by Benjamin Fondane (1928), *Paupières mûres*, *Barre fixe*, and *Mtasipoi*.

production was important up until the mid-1930s. One must notably mention *Pulchérie veut une auto* by Benjamin Péret (1923); *La loi de l'accomodation chez les borgnes* by Picabia (1928), a "film in three parts" that demands of the *reader* to use the screen of his imagination to view the film; the Desnos screenplays, the titles of which refer to the neighborhood places where the surrealist used to hang out (*Les récifs de l'amour, Les mystères du metropolitan*); or *Onésime à Dijon*, which makes reference to the hero of the Gaumont series of comics created between 1912 and 1914 by Jean Durand. These screenplays were made more episodic later (Henri Storck published in 1951 an unfilmed screenplay, *La rue*). Unlike the work of Soupault, a man destined to film his "cinematographic poems" (but without success), many texts by Dali (*Babaouo*, published by Cahiers Libres in 1932), Péret, Desnos, Artaud, Ribemond-Dessaignes, and others were destined only to be read and to "lavish the extraordinary, to multiply anomalies or deformations, to toss the universe around, to ceaselessly speculate about the uncanny and the absurd" (Virmaux, 72). The rather supple form of the texts, ranging from synopsis to dissection, in an era when the publication of screenplays was neither frequent nor institutionalized, offered new potential for writing unstructured texts, free from the constraints and rationality imposed by the narrative or the essay. It also offers the chance to create poetry without writing poems (an exception made in the case of Soupault). But then cinema is only a way of finding and renewing the literary experience.

The number of surrealist films produced seems negligible in comparison to the abundance of screenplays written at the time. Only three films are unanimously recognized: *La coquille et le clergyman* by Germaine Dulac (1927, based on a scenario by Antonin Artaud), *Un chien andalou* by Luis Buñuel (1929, co-written by Salvador Dali), and *L'âge d'or* by Luis Buñuel (1930), the last being an absolute point of reference in the subject of surrealism, in part because of the scandal that it provoked and its subsequent ban,[7] but also because it gave rise to the publication of a "surrealist manifesto concerning *L'âge d'or*" in 1931, the only signed collective text from the movement that truly discussed cinema. The judgment on cinema here is irrevocable:

> From the endless spool of film, proposed to our eyes until now and today dissolved, of which some fragments were only mere entertainment to spend an evening; some others, a subject of dejection and incredible

7. The film remained banned in France until 1981.

cretinization; some others the source of a brief and incomprehensible exaltation. What do we retain if not the arbitrary voice perceived in some of Mack Senett's comedies; the voice of defiance in *Entracte*; that of savage love in *Ombres blanches*; of an equally unlimited hope and despair in Chaplin's films? Aside from this, nothing, except for the irreducible call to revolution in *Le Cuirassé Potemkine*. Nothing besides *Un chien andalou* and *L'âge d'or* which are located beyond all that exists.[8]

Besides these three films, there existed a handful of other works during the 1920s that were similar to surrealist works, but were not recognized as strictly surrealist; some of these were rejected on the grounds that they followed other artistic currents—the rotoreliefs of *Anemic cinema* by Duchamp (1926) borrowed from Dadaist processes, seen in the first two Man Ray films, *Retour à la maison* (1923), presented at a Dada show, and *Emak Bakia* (1927); others, including abstract films, pure cinema, or *Le sang d'un poète* by Cocteau (1928) were condemned by the surrealists; finally *L'étoile de mer* by Man Ray (1929) is often not considered a "surrealist film" because the words, rather than the film itself, are the most important part of the work. Thus it is called "the Desnos poem interpreted by Man Ray."[9] Even without showing the intransigence and rigidity of the attribution of the title "surrealist" to films made before the dissolution of the movement in 1939, one must state that the truly surrealist film is a rare occurrence. It is so rare that it does not authorize a priori the pinpointing of recurrent characteristics inherent to the genre. There are many causes for the paucity of surrealist films: a scarcity of producer-patrons willing to invest in such productions for a rather limited audience; internal ruptures in the surrealist movement; and the impossibility, according to Virmaux, of combining the general ideology of surrealism with the conditions and the length of filming and filmmaking that do not allow for improvisation or spontaneity (Vermaux, 85). The invention of films with sound that is sometimes evoked is a more questionable reason. If Artaud or Breton effectively condemn spoken films by saying that they cause silent films to lose their magic, it wasn't in fact until 1934 that censorship and standardization acted as a brake for experimental cinema.

8. "Manifeste des surréalistes à propos de *L'âge d'or*," reproduced in *L'avant-scène cinéma* 27–28 (June 15–July 15, 1963).

9. On the limits of the body of surrealist films, see Virmaux, *Les surréalistes et le cinéma*, 34–38.

The preceding years are characterized by a great richness of experiments with sound in film, in all sectors of cinematographic production, and sound did not at first create a barrier for members of the avant-garde:[10] *L'âge d'or* is a film with sound and the "interior dialogue" of the two lovers in the park (Lya Lys and Modot) illustrates that sound participates in the construction of the imaginary space and time. The characters carry out a dialogue without opening their mouths and when they move their lips, their motion does not correspond to the words that the viewer hears. While the characters do not leave their seats in the park, their voices blend with Wagner's *Prélude à la mort d'Isolde.* Their dialogue first evokes a conversation murmured between lovers in bed:

> Man: "Are you tired?"
> Young Woman: "I was going to sleep."
> Man: "Where's the button to turn it off?"
> Young Woman: "At the foot of the bed . . . you're hurting me with your elbow."
> Man: "Move your head this way; the pillow is cooler here."
> Young Woman: "Where is your hand? I'm fine like this. Let's stay like this—don't move."
> Man: "Are you cold?"
> Young Woman: "No, I'm falling asleep."
> Man: "Sleep."

The dialogue continues with a passionate declaration by Lya Lys, a character who calls to mind Medea: "I have been waiting for you for a long time. What a joy . . . what a joy to have killed our children!" The pause is filled with the exalted repetition of two words by Modot, "My love, my love, my love, my love . . . , my love." This innovative use of sound allows for both the multiplicity of space and time and the liberation of the strength of mad love off-camera, while the image actually shows us nothing more than the present state of two lovers, who are always prevented in the film from achieving their desires.

## SURREALISM AS A CATEGORY OF INTERPRETATION

But, if truly surrealist films are rare, one consequently witnesses, at least in France, an inflation of the term "surrealist film" to designate

10. See Martin Barnier, *En route vers le parlant. Histoire d'une évolution technologique, économique et esthétique du cinéma (1926–1934)* (Liège: Éditions du Céfal, 2002), 211–15.

films of all kinds, experimental films in commercial cinema coming
from art films that express in a conscious or involuntary way a widespread surrealism or contain fragments of surrealism. Works like those
of Arrabal, that claim to be surrealist; the abundant filmography of
Buñuel after *L'âge d'or*; the films that older surrealists helped to make
(for example Hitchcock's *Spellbound*, because of Dali's contribution to
the dream sequence): all of these are oneiric works that prove the existence of a veritable fantasy in the construction of imaginary worlds,
works in which the subject is a story of passionate or impossible love.
The semantic shift that accompanies the popularization of the term
"surrealist" (that has come to mean in today's French "bizarre" or
"strange") certainly explains this flourishing of surrealist films outside
of surrealism. But Ado Kyrou's *Le surréalisme au cinéma*,[11] published
for the first time in 1963, is likely to be responsible for this situation,
too. Beyond its clearly normative intention (to distinguish between
films that express, even in a transient manner, an authentic surrealism
and those that only produce a pale reflection of it), this book, starting
from the principle that "cinema is essentially surrealist," "that the
dreams of a sleeping person lose their nature of dreams . . . in order to
turn before our marveled eyes into reality" (Kyrou, 9), ends up finding
surrealism to be, if not everywhere, in any case in an impressive number of films that address "love" or "revolt," that capture "elsewhere"
or "the impossible" (these are titles of Kyrou's chapters), or in films that
embody a sort of "pre-surrealism" (Méliès, Feuillade). Nearly the first
two thirds of the book are dedicated to films that "redivide at one point
the luminous line of surrealism" (Kyrou, 169). That these meetings
with surrealism are often completely involuntary matters very little to
Kyrou. On the contrary even, this "objective coincidence" would tend
implicitly to give even more value to the magnetizing moments that
came from it: "Today involuntary surrealism, following from old
habits, is hidden under the strangest tawdry rags whether in filmed bal-
lets, in the dreams of average films, or in advertisements one sees during intermission, the magnetic spirit of surrealism slaps numb spectators in the face and revives them" (Kyrou, 169).

One thus comes upon a paradoxical situation where there is, on the
one hand, a minuscule group of surrealist films that are the expression
of the aesthetic movement in cinema, and, on the other, an abundance

11. Ado Kyrou, *Le surréalisme au cinéma* (Paris: Ramsay Poche Cinéma, 1985
[1963]).

of films in which fragments are read as surrealist and therefore labeled as surrealist films. It is the existence of this last type of surrealist film that causes one to think that surrealism functions today as a genre, in other words, an *a posteriori* category that allows for the regrouping of a certain number of works (any work of which a fragment, aspect, or element can be labeled as surrealist). The reference to surrealism ends up designating here "what we collectively believe it to be," to go back to a definition of genre by Andrew Tudor.[12] Tudor makes this proposition after having underlined (in the case of the "Western" movies) that critics always start from an implicit and common definition of the genre they are studying, which indeed determines a body of works, and that they redefine the genre afterwards according to their original hypothesis. He therefore identifies an unconsciously tautological approach, in which he substitutes a recursive definition that insists upon the interpretative consensus presiding over the recognition of a genre and the distribution of a film in a generic category. Each interpretative community fashions and uses its own generic categories, according to its own strategies, its experience of cinema, of culture, its time period, and its place in society. To separate films into genres by using the very rigorous, pragmatic perspective developed by Rick Altman in *Film/Genre*[13] is to do much more than map out the world of cinematographic works or to pinpoint on which continent a film is found: it is to express, activate, or accept a system of common and implicit references, a "labeling game," as Jean-Pierre Esquenazi calls it,[14] which departs from the "language games" described by Wittgenstein in his *Philosophical Investigations*, that primarily resulted in patterns of production and reception. Therefore, the genre has to be considered above all as a category of interpretation. This category actually says more about the relation to cinema and culture of the one who recognizes and mobilizes it than about the films that it characterizes. From this perspective, the genre designates a category, supposedly well known, common, and shared, that one can associate with a film in order to characterize it even if it is not a genre film. It has the merit of separating the cinematographic genre from the pejorative meaning that was mentioned at the

12. Andrew Tudor, "Genre" [1974], in *Film Genre Reader II*, ed. Barry Keith Grant (Austin: University of Texas Press, 1995), 5.

13. Rick Altman, *Film/Genre* (London: BFI, 1999).

14. Jean-Pierre Esquenazi, "Le renouvellement d'un jeu de langage. Genres et canaux," *Réseaux* 81, "Les genres télévisuels" (Paris: CNET, January–February 1997), 105.

beginning of this article. It also provides a more widespread and less taxonomic sense to the notion of genre, since any category that enables viewers (but also producers, critics, and others) to name and then situate a particular film can be considered a genre. Since it is an interpretative category, it becomes a mediating tool between works and their public.[15]

While recent theories of genre focus on this communicative and pragmatic function, one can hesitate to use the term "genre" in the sense that in abandoning the traditional conception of classification, one expands upon the sense that one usually hears about. Some authors, including Jean-Marie Schaeffer, consequently prefer to discuss *genericity*.[16] I propose to discuss *generic operators* in order to designate categories that, without listing genres in dictionaries and without departing from "genre names," have ceased to function as expressions of the aesthetic movement (or, in other cases, having to do with the technique or the production of a work), but have become categories of interpretation.[17] This is precisely the case with "surrealist film," and the surrealist movement is not the only one concerned with this genrification, which is certainly an indicator of major cultural diffusion, but also is an indicator of a stereotypical reduction. In fact, as indicated by Jacqueline Nacache,

> The New Wave as a generic operator is no longer an artistic label but a category of interpretation that is valued less for its content than for its function. In this, the interpretive category not only rejoins the genre through its capacity as mediator, but it also assures it almost more effectively than the artistic label. For if the criteria of genericity have evolved so much that today's spectator does not really know what to expect from a Western or a musical, the "New Wave" or "young French

15. Raphaëlle Moine, *Les genres du cinéma* (Paris: Nathan, 2002), 19–20 and 83–85.

16. Jean-Marie Schaeffer, *Qu'est-ce qu'un genre littéraire* (Paris: Editions du Seuil), 1989.

17. The "remake," for example, that initially indicates a technique of production of film works starting with a preexisting work, functions in French criticism as a "generic operator"; in the postmodern era of recycling old films, at the time of Hollywood remakes of foreign films, these works are evaluated (and compared to their source, often negatively) based on their qualities and flaws. The remake has become a mediation that constructs a horizon and critical reception posture *a priori*. It is similar to novelization. *Cf.* Raphaëlle Moine, "Cinéma, genres et novellisation," in Jan Baetens and Marc Litts, *La novellisation/Novelization. Du film au livre/From Film to Novel* (Leuven: Leuven University Press, 2004), 87.

cinema" labels are by contrast loaded with connotations that do not need to be elucidated in order to be understood."[18]

## THE GENRIFICATION OF SURREALIST FILM

How is surrealist film able to constitute a generic operator? What does this genrification constitute, and what does it preserve from the surrealism of the surrealists? To answer these questions, it is relevant to examine the occurrences and the use of the term "surrealist film." In this regard, the critical reception of films offers good territory to investigate. As an example, I will use an entire corpus of film reviews that appeared in France between December 2004 and January 2005 in the weekly *Télérama*, a French cultural magazine with a readership made up of people of the educated middle-class—neither a newspaper for the masses nor a publication strictly for cinephiles like the *Cahiers du cinéma*. Four reviews make reference to surrealist film—the review of *Dias de campo* (a Chilean film by Raoul Ruiz, reviewed by Jacques Morice in issue 2866 on December 18, 2004), the review of *Et les lâches s'agenouillent* (a Canadian film by Guy Maddin, reviewed by François Gorin in issue 2868 on January 1, 2005), the review of *Château ambulant* (a Japanese film by Hayao Miyazaki, reviewed by Cécile Mury in issue 2870 on January 15, 2005), and finally the review of the new commercial showing of *Pandora and the Flying Dutchman* (Albert Lewin, Great Britain, 1951, reviewed by Guillemette Olivier in issue 2868). The first observation: "surrealist film" is used to characterize four very different films. The reasons that prompt critics to make reference to surrealism are also very diverse, but they are rather representative of what constitutes a "surrealist film" in contemporary France. The reasons given are above all thematic—the strange object that makes up the castle in the Miyazaki film ("a giant with the look of a chicken, infernal machinery, a delirium of intricate devices and passageways, of traps, valves and bolts"), as well as the love binding Sophie and Hauru the magician, described as "the antithesis of all Disney floweriness." For *Pandora*, it is the myth of the Flying Dutchman who wanders in search of "THE woman," and also the baroque style of the décor, the lighting and the colors that beautify Ava Gardner. One finds here again

18. Jacqueline Nacache, "Nouvelle vague et jeune cinéma: des 'opérateurs génériques' à la genrification du cinéma français," in *Le cinéma français face aux genres*, ed. Raphaëlle Moine (Paris: AFRHC, 2005), 61.

the equation "mad love + exaltation of feminine beauty = surrealism," already used by Kyrou in order to find aspects of surrealism in the Lewin film: "The two hands united in Pandora's fishnet are a conclusion full of consequences and the stunning Ava Gardner, who personifies the eternal lover of the flying Dutchman, is for me the perfect example of a woman in love. Lewin highlighted throughout his entire film the predestination of a great love. As a cultivated and intelligent man (and as an aesthete too), he proclaimed his fierce faith in love" (Kyrou, 129). It is once more love and death that authorizes François Gorin to discuss the "surrealist film" in the case of *Et les lâches s'agenouillent*, but in this case the experimental character of the autobiographical film reinforces this characterization: "There is sound, but no words. A trembling Super-8 image, in black and white, colored adequately here and there. Thus the blue hands of the dead father of a young woman who turns the life of hockey player Guy upside down, a woman who will eventually have these hands transplanted onto her lover in order to satisfy a vengeance. A magician's trick, in fact, that mirrors this minor film, a melodrama that deviates toward a surrealist tale." As for the Ruiz film, "a nostalgic meditation on the mother country and the fleeting years," it is judged to be surrealist because of the past works of the director, often attributed with a Buñuelian affiliation, and because of its complex structure that allows for the realization of parallel and communicating worlds: "a typical Ruiz movie, as one says, the promise of these narrative loops that the most surrealist of our directors executes as effortlessly as if he were breathing. There are also tales independent of the main action, a back-and-forth between the kingdom of the dead and the world of the living, but with transparency and unusual simplicity."

These four readings that mobilize the generic operator of the "surrealist film" seem to me to be rather representative of what the surrealist film has become in the field of contemporary criticism. They bring surrealism back to semantic traits (passionate, heterosexual love, a diegetic, oneiric, unrealistic or imaginary universe that excludes all realistic representation) and/or syntactical traits (the meandering story in which the complex time structure offers, in the words of Gilles Deleuze, "a plurality of simultaneous worlds," "a simultaneity of presents in different worlds"[19]). When one knows that it is mainly the stable combination of semantic and syntactical elements that allows one,

19. Gilles Deleuze, *L'image-temps* (Paris: Éditions de Minuit, 1985), 135.

from an academic point of view, to recognize the existence of strong genres and to analyze them as such, one sees that the genrification of film is actually very advanced! Of course, genrification proceeds from a simplification that is explained by the diffusion and popularity of a surrealist vulgate, all artistic practices combined. But in the case of cinema, it also comes from definitions given by the surrealists themselves and from the weakness of their theoretical discourse on the seventh art. As I mentioned previously regarding the unfilmable screenplays and the weakness of the strictly surrealist body of works, and as Claude Murcia remarks, "in general their relation with cinema—which denies the worldliness of the text in order to search in film only for the brief instances susceptible to trigger excitation or *rêverie*—scarcely goes along with the sense of real interest for cinematographic work."[20] Cinema appeared to the surrealists as above all a new art, a language that could abolish all constraints, a writing in which everything is permissible. Well before Edgar Morin and his *Cinéma ou l'homme imaginaire* (1956), the surrealists seemed convinced, as spectators more than filmmakers, that a certain magical logic was shared by cinematic images and oneiric images. For example, Antonin Artaud, while pondering cinematic genius, writes that it is "essentially revealing of a secret life to which it is directly related," and that it is made "to express aspects of thought, the interior of the conscience, not so much by playing with images but by something more unpredictable that restores them to us with their direct material, without interposition, without representation."[21] Because of this, he champions a "cinema studded with dreams that gives us the sensation of pure life."[22] The writings by members of the surrealist group generally confirm this: to them cinema is "a wonderful way of expressing dreams,"[23] in other words, a way to attain surreality, a place where the contradictions between reality and dream are resolved. In the late 1920s, Buñuel was in total agreement with the surrealist group in terms of the relationship between film and dreams, even though he later claimed never to have taken part in the slightly naïve enthusiasm that inspired these particular possibilities in cinema. The future director thus did not distinguish himself from his avant-

20. Claude Murcia, *Un chien andalou, L'âge d'or. Étude critique* (Paris: Nathan, Synopsis, 1994), 18.

21. Antonin Artaud, "Surréalisme et cinéma," cited in *Études cinématographiques* 38–39 (Paris: Mignard-Les Lettres Modernes, 1965), 123.

22. Artaud, *Avant-Propos de La coquille et le clergyman* (Paris: NRF, 1927).

23. Philippe Soupault, "Entretien," *Études cinématographiques* 38–39 (n.d.).

garde companions when he undertook with Dali the writing and filming of *Un chien andalou* by joining their two dreams. His aim was to
reinstate the "storm of dreams that floods sleep in waves," to extract
from nothingness some of these "billions and billions of images that
surge every night and dissipate almost right away, enveloping the earth
in a cloak of lost dreams."[24] The purpose of *Un chien andalou* is very
clear, indeed: to use the logic of the unconscious to put into words
dreams and fantasies according to an associative logic, to unite dream
and reality, consciousness and unconsciousness, apart from all symbolism. Two antagonistic series resulted from this, one evoking desire
(the sea urchin, the box, the hair, the breasts, the buttocks . . . ) the
other castration (the fall, the razor, the cut hand, the obliteration of the
mouth . . . ). The figures of displacement, of analogy, and of condensa-
tion govern the discourse and the film. Facing such insistence on joining cinema and dream, one will not be surprised that this oneiric quality, whether in the content of the film or in its form, has today become
a synonym of surrealism. Finally, the famous "Manifeste des surréalistes à propos de *L'âge d'or*" emphasizes themes a great deal (love, and
at a more psychoanalytical level, the conflicts between "the life and the
death instincts") and a subversive way of treating its subjects, but falls
short of providing *cinematographic surrealism* with a clearly defined
aesthetic program.

All of this authorizes a later stereotypical reduction of surrealism
around a thematic nucleus (the representations of the imaginary, im-
pulses, love and desire) that can come to be embodied in a narrative
form, certainly supple and perplexing, but relatively codified after all
(the stratification of the film narrative in sequences, parallel times and
worlds). Is is therefore not surprising that the term "surrealist film" is
used primarily in regard to the fantasy genre that frequently relies on
the same themes and the same type of storytelling. The "generic operator" of surrealist film thus serves on one hand to delimit a sort of sub-
genre within the important galaxy of fantasy films, regardless of the actual influence of surrealism on their authors. On the other hand, by
superimposing itself onto a usual generic denomination, the generic
operator helps to extract works from the field of commercial cinema,
to take them out of the field of popular culture, and to give them cultural value. Fantasy films, while called "surrealist films," are received,
presented, and interpreted with the help of a nobler and more artistic

24. Luis Buñuel, *Mon dernier soupir* (Paris: Ramsay Poche Cinéma, 1982), 111–12.

category. David Lynch films, which are often referred to as surrealist, can thus be seen as artistic and personal films rather than as genre films. They are undoubtedly both, but surrealism serves here to bring the aesthetic qualities of film to the forefront. The interpenetration of space and time, the substitution of characters, the structure in the form of a Moebius strip where different worlds revolve in a loop without ever fully overlapping, the "schizophrenia," where it is impossible to decide whether it is that of the heroes or that of the story, allow one, from the television series *Twin Peaks* to *Mulholland Drive* and *Lost Highway*, to read these films as surrealist films and eventually as original works. To label a film as surrealist is therefore to re-establish a strategy of "distinction" (in the sociological sense that Bourdieu gave to the term), as one sees in the previously cited review of *Château ambulant*. Its author discusses "surrealist film" by emphasizing that the love story is not syrupy-sweet like in animated Hollywood films. The article's introduction proceeds in the same way: "all of the genius of Miyazaki concentrated in a surrealist fable that twists manga and fairy tales." One thus falls victim to a sort of circular reasoning, where it is difficult to know if the film is becoming surrealist because it moves away from normed forms (the word "surrealism" being a shortcut for communicating subversion and the distortion of genres, constraints, and codes) or because one is eager to show that it moves away from standard production. So, to interpret *Le château ambulant* as a surrealist film is to define it at the same time as an anti-Disney and an anti-manga film, or, in other words, as a work that opposes the two dominant types of animated films in popular culture.

Surrealism attributed to this or that film functions as an indicator of "authorship"[25] that accentuates the artistic and personal dimension of the work. The example of fantasy films illustrates this well, but it is also noticeable outside of the genre. The case of *Le charme discret de la bourgeoisie* (1972) seems to me to be particularly enlightening. Buñuel's return to surrealism, seen in this film and its successor in

---

25. I am borrowing this term from Esquenazi, who used it in regard to Godard to indicate how the theorization of the politics of authors by the Young Turks of *Cahiers du cinéma* brings them, when they become directors, to "make evident in their films, at any cost, the idea that dominates their personality and organizes their work." This imperative of authorship expresses the will to support a posture of the artist. It has been repeated many times since then—successfully, one might add—as a criterion of aesthetic judgment by the cinephilic press. See Jean-Pierre Esquenazi, *Godard et la société française des années 1960* (Paris: Armand-Colin, 2004), 58–63.

Buñuel's filmography (*Le fantôme de la liberté,* 1974) has been discussed at length, but when the film was released, criticism hesitated
between two interpretations of it. As Jean-Pierre Esquenazi showed
while studying the French critical reception of the film at the time,
readings sometimes emphasized the satirical dimension and pamphle-
teering of the film (it is therefore a caricature, successful or not, of members of the bourgeoisie who flaunt their title), and sometimes the
oneiric dimension (it is in this case added on to the aesthetic universe
of its author and to Buñuelian surrealism).[26] Let us recall the principle
of the film, constructed around the repetition of a meal shared by the
six main protagonists, always left unfinished because of the occurrence
of events, each more bizarre than the last. These repeated and fruitless
attempts provide unity for the story that constantly blurs the line between dream and reality. The various unsuccessful meals provide the
subject of an acerbic social portrayal, pointed to by the title and discussed in some articles at the time by critics who did not fail to notice
this aspect of the film. The bourgeoisie of the film is hypocritical, idle,
and unproductive. Consumers (often frustrated) of food, drink, sex, and
drugs are addressees of someone else's stories—the ambassador Don
Rafaël, the Sénéchal couple, Madame Thévenot, her husband and her
sister Florence—who do nothing except ensure the permanence of a
constantly interrupted ritual. While they are the main characters, they
are never exactly actors or trustees of a personal or family story that the
secondary characters of the film have the privilege to possess. The
repetitive cycle directed by Buñuel in the film encloses these pure social types in a strict circle of social membership: three men who take
part in shady business deals and don't hesitate to use violence in order
to continue doing this business, while the women meet at tea time.
Moreover, the bourgeois décor, meticulously recreated on screen by the
director, is, metaphorically but also literally in one scene, a theater
stage on which the bourgeoisie maintains its position in society by
playing its role. That is why *Le charme discret de la bourgeoisie* is full
of various codified words: expressions of politeness, ritual meal-time
conversational expressions, menu or recipe terms, proverbial truths,
well-known clichés or altered ones. When the film is interpreted as a
satire of the bourgeoisie (a great social obsession in France after May

26. See Esquenazi, "Répétitions bourgeoises," *Buñuel, siglo XXI*, ed. Isabel Santao-
lalla (Saragosse: Institución Fernando el Catolico/Prensas Universitarias de Zaragoza,
2004), 111–21.

1968), it is its capacity to account for the world it makes reference to that is put forward instead of Buñuel the author himself. In this case, the sequences of walks in the countryside that punctuate the film are interpreted as metaphors of the insignificance or the emptiness incarnated by the bourgeoisie. But *Le charme discret de la bourgeoisie* does not simply alternate between unfinished meals and disturbing events: it almost inextricably intertwines dream and reality in order to do so. The dream makes its appearance at the fourth unachieved meal in the form of a "retelling of a dream," which can be easily isolated. While the army conducting field exercises occupies the home of the Sénéchals, a sergeant, having just brought news to the colonel, tells the dinner guests one of his dreams, morbid and perfectly stereotypical. The sergeant's dream opens the floodgates of the imagination in the film and, starting with this sequence, real and imaginary are no longer distinguishable. Dreams are thus neither circumscribed nor easily identified by their aesthetics, and the principle of an *a posteriori* discovery of the imaginary status of these scenes becomes generalized. What the viewer believes to be reality topples over on two occasions in the dream. The meal hosted by the colonel, the masquerade on a theater stage, is nothing but Sénéchal's dream and the "second" meal at the colonel's, which the viewer thought to be "the real one," turns out to have been dreamt by Thévenot who had been dreaming the film . . . for some time. According to the same principle, in the police station sequences where the *bourgeois* are held, the episode of the bloody brigadier, that a flashback falsely authenticates, is nothing but a product of the imagination of the officer. The screenplay engages in a final pirouette after the general massacre at the very end of the film—Don Rafaël wakes up sweating and starving. Could the entire film be the dream of a hungry man? Critics who favor this labyrinth of dreams underline thus the surrealism of *Le charme discret de la bourgeoisie* and these oneiric interpretations free the film of all possible connections with the social and cultural world. They instead associate the film with the imaginary, conceived as autonomous, of Buñuel the author, a true incarnation of surrealism on screen.

The ideal but all too rarely used surrealist instrument, cinema, has likely become, like other artistic and cultural productions, a place where influences, often widespread and unconscious, manifest themselves. They stemmed from surrealism after it reached its peak as an aesthetic movement. Directors were most definitely influenced by surrealism (some very profoundly, like Buñuel, above all a "historic sur-realist" before distancing himself from the group). But here, instead, I wanted to highlight the influence of surrealism on the critics' view of films (and on the view of all of us, too). It is this second influence that caused the transformation of "surrealist film" into a generic operator. In this sense, if cinema constitutes an otherness of surrealism because it is a mode of expression that was only occasionally explored by the surrealists, films labeled as surrealist today also appear as "others" in relation to the surrealist project. Indeed, these films only join the genre after surrealism has been simplified and institutionalized as a truly modern label of artistic quality.

—Translated by Pierre Taminiaux

# GEORGIANA M. M. COLVILE

# Between Surrealism and Magic Realism: The Early Feature Films of André Delvaux

> Ici a commencé pour moi ce que j'appellerai l'épanchement du songe dans la vie réelle.
> —Gérard de Nerval[1]

> Réel et imaginaire, . . . s'affrontent sans se concilier ni se réconcilier. De cet affrontement naît l'entre-deux: précisément l'oeuvre. . . . Ce pays de l'entre-deux, qui ne réussit à recouvrer son unité que dans l'imaginaire devenu langage: dans *l'oeuvre*, c'est le pays où je vis.
> —André Delvaux[2]

Poetry, magic, erotic longing, and the omnipresence of death pervade André Delvaux's carefully crafted fiction films, hence their success at international film festivals, his lasting reputation with intellectual audiences in France, and his fame as the Master of Belgian cinema in his own country.[3] His first feature film, the 1965 *L'homme au crâne rasé* (The Man with his Hair Cut Short),[4] adapted from the eponymous novel[5] by Johan Daisne, the main literary representative of Flemish magic realism, immediately struck French viewers as a revival of the

1. "Then began for me what I will call the flow of dream into reality." Gérard de Nerval, *Aurélia* (1855). All translations in this essay are mine.
2. "Here the real and the imaginary confront each other [as opposites] and are never reconciled. An in-between state is born of that confrontation: precisely the work of art. . . . That country of the in-between that can only recover its unity within the imaginary as it becomes language: within the *work of art*, that's the country I inhabit." André Delvaux, "Cinéma francophone de Belgique" in *André Delvaux,* ed. Adolphe Nysenholc (Brussels: Editions de l'Université de Bruxelles, 1994), 43.
3. See "Mort du maître du cinéma belge: André Delvaux." [Obituary for André Delvaux]. A. de Baeque, *Libération,* October 7, 2002.
4. *De man die zijn haar kort liet knippen* (1965), a Belgian production, shot in Flemish, French subtitles, BW, 35mm, 1h34 min.
5. Johan Daisne, *De man die zijn haar kort liet knippen* (Brussels and The Hague: A. Manteau N.V., 1948). French translation by Maddy Buysse, *L'homme au crâne rasé* (Paris: Albin Michel, 1965).

**YFS 109,** *Surrealism and Its Others,* ed. Katharine Conley and Pierre Taminiaux, © 2006 by Yale University.

spirit of surrealism. The film obtained prizes in seven countries, including the London British Film Institute Prize for best film of the year and the Grand Prix Khalimer at the 1966 Festival du Jeune Cinéma at Hyères, where Jean-Luc Godard "stood up in the midst of the audience to pay tribute to an unknown director's film."[6]

On October 4, 2002, Delvaux delivered a self-critical "testamentary" lecture at a world conference on the arts in Valencia, Spain, minutes before he died of a heart attack. It was titled "Un cinéma éclaté dans une Belgique éclatée" (A Divided Cinema in a Divided Belgium).[7] He expressed guilt for having privileged formal and aesthetic perfectionism over sociopolitical ideology in his early films (especially concerning the Belgian language conflict) and sadly admitted his ideal of a common Flemish and Francophone (Wallon) "Belgitude" to be more myth than reality. He concluded by recommending cultural "métissage." He had only devoted one film, *Femme entre chien et loup* (1979),[8] to Belgium's political split, although the language problem had been woven into the poetic fabric of *Un soir, un train* (1968). Nevertheless, Delvaux promoted a Belgian national cinema, and inaugurated and taught film classes at the Institut National Supérieur des Arts et du Spectacle from its opening in 1963.

Jacques Mandelbaum pinpoints in *L'homme au crâne rasé* the double tendency toward surrealism and magic realism that characterizes most of Delvaux's fiction films, calling it "an impassive hymn to mad love [ . . . with] a touch of surrealist cruelty and strangeness, drawn from the depths of the Flemish tradition of the fantastic, while appropriating . . . a 'whiteness' typical of Bresson"[9] and, incidentally, of André Breton's imagery in *L'amour fou*.[10] As we shall see, Delvaux was a deliberate magic realist, on his own terms, and a more reluctant latter-day surrealist. In this essay, I will explore both dimensions in Delvaux's four early fiction features: *L'homme au crâne rasé* (1965); *Un soir, un train* (1968); *Rendez-vous à Bray* (1971) and *Belle* (1973).

6. Adolphe Nysenholc, "De la vie à l'oeuvre," in *André Delvaux*, ed. Nysenholc, 16.

7. Reproduced in its entirety in *Le monde*, November 19, 2002.

8. "Femme entre chien et loup" literally means "Woman Between Dog and Wolf" and figuratively signifies "In the Twilight Zone." As a historical film, it stands apart from Delvaux's other features.

9. Jacques Mandelbaum, "André Delvaux: une oeuvre liée au réalisme magique," *Le monde*, October 8, 2002.

10. See Georgiana M. M. Colvile, "Breton caresse les ours blancs: du surréalisme, du désir et des nuages," *Mélusine* XXV (February 2005): 231–46, regarding André Breton's *L'amour fou* (Paris, Gallimard, 1937), clouds, and the color white.

Actual surrealist films, produced by members of Breton's group, proved rare, as still do their critical assessments, none of which mention Delvaux,[11] whereas every book on Delvaux refers to surrealism. Henri Béhar titles his introduction to a 2004 issue of *Mélusine* on *Le cinéma des surréalistes*,[12] "L'inadaptation cinématographique." He quotes contradictory statements by a range of surrealists and film critics, from Breton, for whom Buñuel and Dali's *Un chien andalou* (An Andalusian Dog - 1928) and *L'âge d'or* (1930) were the only surrealist films, to Jean Goudal, Ado Kyrou et al., who regarded film as the surrealist medium par excellence. Béhar also provides film historians' official top ten surrealist films (10–11).[13] There were cult films, too, such as Feuillade's *Fantômas* series (1913–1914), Murnau's *Nosferatu* (1922), Eisenstein's *Potemkin* (1925), Chaplin's early comedies (1915–1928), Hathaway's *Peter Ibbetson* (1935), and so on. The surrealists considered cinemas as entertainment places, where they could glean new poetic images or associations, like the flea-market. They wrote unused screenplays,[14] as did Delvaux, notably "Le collier de Sybilla: Une aventure d'Arsène Lupin,"[15] which emulates the Fantômas films. Officially surrealist Belgian films prove even rarer. Most of them revolve around Magritte, like Pierre Livet's 1929 *Les fleurs meurtries* (Bruised Flowers), and Delvaux's work is no more mentioned in that context than in the French one.[16]

Unlike surrealism, which Breton kept redefining in his manifestoes and elsewhere, magic realism resists precise description and remains known for its "multiplicity of imprecisions and differences,"[17] partly because it "incorporates eight languages and five continents" (214).

11. Including the recent and very complete *Surréalisme et cinéma,* ed. G. A. Astre and Y. Kovacs (Paris: Minard, 2000).

12. *Mélusine* XXIV (February 2004): 9–13.

13. In addition to the two Buñuel films: René Clair's *Entr'acte* (1927), Man Ray's *Retour à la raison* (1923), Emak Bakia (1927) and *L'étoile de mer* (poem by Desnos, 1928), Germaine Dulac's *La coquille et le clergyman* (script by Artaud, 1928), *La perle* (script by Hugnet, 1928), Man Ray and Duchamp's *Le mystère du château de dé* (1929), and Michel Zimbacca and J. L. Bédouin's *L'invention du monde* (1951).

14. See *Anthologie du cinéma invisible,* ed. Christian Janicot (Paris: Jean-Michel Place, 1995).

15. Co-authored with Marcel Croes in 1972 and published in *Les cahiers du scénario* 2/3 (Brussels: Winter, Summer 1987): 35–111.

16. See "Cinéma et surréalisme en Belgique" in *Surréalismes en Belgique,* ed. Paul Aron, Special issue of *Textyles* 8 (November 1991): 269–81.

17. Jean Weisgerber, "Bilan provisoire," in *Le réalisme magique: roman-peinture-cinéma* (Brussels: Université de Bruxelles, L'âge d'homme, 1987), 214.

Under the influence of specific nineteenth-century Symbolist, Fantastic, or Realist authors such as "Poe, Baudelaire ("La chambre double"),[18] Hispanic-American 'modernismo,' Henry James, Kubin, Apollinaire and Pirandello, it first takes shape in Germany and Italy in the 1920s" (Weisgerber, 214). Its main practitioners include Franz Roh and Ernst Jünger (Germany), Massimo Bontempelli and Giorgio de Chirico (Italy), Jorges Luis Borges, Bioy Casarès, Gabriel Garcia Marquez, and Julio Cortazar (Latin America) and, from the 1940s, Johan Daisne (Flemish Belgium).[19] Fabien S. Gérard defines Belgian magic realism as an "aesthetic tendency, both pictorial and literary" (91) and inextricably bound up with André Delvaux. Furthermore, it is "in no way a revolutionary movement" (Weisgerber, 7). The term was finally coined by Daisne (Weisgerber, 17), and for his first two feature films, *L'homme au crâne rasé* and *Un soir, un train*,[20] Delvaux chose to adapt texts by that author.

Although Delvaux admired Daisne's writing, his approach to the subject matter was radically different in his adaptations and he devised his own cinematic magic realism. Adolphe Nysenholc applies the expression "L'alchimie de l'adaptation" (Nysenholc 1994, 267) to Delvaux's final feature, *L'oeuvre au noir* (1988), from Marguerite Yourcenar's 1968 novel about a sixteenth-century alchemist, but all his fiction films (except *Femme entre chien et loup*), seem to transpose Rimbaud's "verbal Alchemy," a favorite surrealist concept, onto the screen. Daisne's novel *L'homme au crâne rasé* conveys an "inner reality," through the interminable stream of consciousness confession of his disturbed protagonist Govert Miereveld, in which reality, the imaginary, hallucinations, and delirium merge. Govert, a meek lawyer and teacher, first relates his unrequited passion for Fran, a beautiful student, and his pathetic attempts to attract her attention at graduation; next he describes a horrific autopsy he witnessed ten years later, followed by a chance encounter with Fran, then a diva, her narrative of sexual disillusion, and his shooting her at her own request (or so he believes). The story ends at the lunatic asylum where Govert tells his tale and finally finds peace after seeing Fran on television, though neither

18. "The Double Room" (1862), meaning real and imaginary, in *Petits poèmes en prose* (Paris: Gallimard, 1973), 28–30.

19. See Adolphe Nysenholc, *André Delvaux ou les visages de l'imaginaire* (Brussels: Éditions de l'Université de Bruxelles, 1985), 91–96.

20. From the short story "De trein der Traagheid" (The Train of Inertia), inspired by another "Egbertha in der Onderweld."

he nor the reader ever find out the date of the program, nor, consequently, whether he had killed her or not. The reader remains distanced
from the deranged but harmless hero and the so-called *magic* aspect of
the novel eludes us. The kindly asylum director is no Caligari[21] and
Govert's sad but moral story remains *realist* from within and without,
as Daisne fuses both levels into one seamless reality.

Magic does emanate from Delvaux's image- and soundtracks. Far
from a naïve first film, *L'homme au crâne rasé* was highly professional,
Delvaux having previously produced ten educational documentary
shorts.[22] The sophisticated magic-realist structure he kept developing
in his later fiction films after *Femme entre chien et loup*, is already present in *L'homme au crâne rasé*. Delvaux described his method in several essays[23] and Laurc Borgomano has analyzed its workings in each
film.[24] First, the protagonist's single subjective focalisation shapes the
whole film; secondly, a structure specific to each feature expresses the
conflict and doubling between the real and imaginary levels of the diegesis; thirdly, the presence and recurrence of various objects provide the
protagonist with clues concerning the ambiguous "reality" of his adventure; fourthly, music plays an active part in Delvaux's plots and often replaces dialogue in whole sequences. Delvaux himself studied music and was an accomplished pianist. His "réalisme magique" could be
termed "réalisation magique" (magic *mise en scène*), being based on
structure and technique.

Concerning the impact of surrealism on Delvaux, I have detected
three dimensions: the one he himself acknowledged, the traces determined by critics, and my own perception of it on the level of content.
As my epigraph shows, Delvaux lived in the "other country" of his
*oeuvre*, much like François Truffaut, to whom directing meant re-

21. In Wiene's 1920 film, *The Cabinet of Dr. Caligari*, a mental patient tells a tale of
persecution by a criminal mountebank, Caligari, who turns out to be the same person as
the asylum director. Caligari, later compared to the Nazis by Siegfried Kracauer, also represents the surrealist's view of psychiatrists!

22. Later, Delvaux shot five other documentaries: *Met Dieric Bouts* (1975), about a
medieval Dutch painter; *To Woody Allen, from Europe with Love* (1980); *Pelléas et
Mélisande* (1984) and *Babel Opéra* (1985), about the staging of two operas; and his last
movie, *1001 Films* (1989), an eight-minute short about the Brussels Cinémathèque.

23. See Delvaux's essays in *André Delvaux ou les visages de l'imaginaire* (1985), in
particular Nysenholc's collage of quotes "Delvaux par lui-même" (97–113), and *André
Delvaux* (1994).

24. Laure Borgomano, "Le réalisme magique," in *André Delvaux une oeuvre—un
film: L'oeuvre au noir*, ed. Borgomano and Nysenholc (Brussels: Éditions Labor and Méri-
diens Klincksieck, 1988), 32–73.

arranging life according to his dreams or fantasies and prolonging his childhood games,[25] as in Freud's theory of "The poet and daydreaming."[26] They were of the same generation, with a similar nostalgia for the nineteenth century, a period when people had time for daydreaming or *"onirisme diurne."*[27] Truffaut especially loved Balzac, while Delvaux, like the surrealists, admired Nerval and Rimbaud.

Delvaux's is a cinema of synaesthesia, in which literature, music, and painting all play an important part. He related to surrealism mainly through painting. Foreign audiences who had never heard of Daisne were quick to detect the impact of Magritte and Paul Delvaux on his early work. He had known Magritte and was consciously influenced by the uncanny spatial juxtapositions in the latter's paintings, which he realized could be transposed temporally into film (Nysenholc 1994, 175–76). Delvaux was reluctant to agree with those who linked his work to non-Belgian surrealists like Breton or de Chirico (175). Incidentally, the Belgian surrealists included music in their activities, while their French counterparts followed Breton in dismissing it as an inferior art.[28]

To my mind, Delvaux's surrealism emerges from the level of the signified or content and could be perceived as the unconscious of his work, while his carefully elaborated magic realist structures constitute its signifier and conscious. Let us now look at the first four films. The opening shots of *L'homme au crâne rasé* combine both levels. Close-ups of Govert's (Senne Rouffaer) face, eyes "wide-shut," then opening, his voice calling "Fran~!" and a reverse close-up shot of her face and elusive gaze, establish his subjective focalisation (Borgomano, 37–38). Furthermore, the eyes opening up might be read as an intertextual reference to the initial shots of *An Andalusian Dog*, when Buñuel slits a woman's eyeball with a razor as though to reveal another, surreal visual dimension, into which the viewer is being invited. Govert's voice is heard off-screen, dissociated from his silent face, while conjuring up Fran's (Beata Tyszkiewicz), so that the two levels of reality (Govert

25. François Truffaut, *Le plaisir des yeux* (Paris: Cahiers du Cinéma, 1987), 245.

26. Sigmund Freud, *Creativity and the Unconscious* (New York: Harper Colophon Books, 1958), 44–54.

27. Henri Agel and Joseph Marty apply this term to the surrealists and to André Delvaux in *André Delvaux de l'inquiétante étrangeté à l'itinéraire initiatique* (Lausanne: L'âge d'homme, 1996), 22.

28. See Robert Wangermée, "Les musiciens du surréalisme bruxellois et l'esprit Dada," in *Surréalismes en Belgique.* Special issue of *Textyles* 8 (November 1991): 257–68.

waking up at home, his wife helping him dress for graduation) and imagination/fantasy (the domain of Fran and Govert's obsessive surrealist "mad love") co-exist. The same double structure prevails during graduation and especially throughout the autopsy scene, which for the doctor and his assistants is routine work, while Govert's horror at the proximity of death becomes palpable to the spectator. Delvaux uses sound and objects to achieve this double effect. The medical professor works inside a tomb, with his arms and instruments hidden from Govert and the audience, while his activity remains unpleasantly audible, for example the scraping of a shinbone. The similarity between the sets of instruments Govert encounters in what Delvaux calls the film's three blocks (Nysenholc 1985, 97–98): a hairdresser's utensils in the first part, the doctor's equipment in the second, and Govert's carpentry tools at the asylum in the third, creates an uncanny effect and reinforces the double magic realist structure. Daisne maintained that Govert had really killed Fran but was sent the merciful illusion of her survival by God (Delvaux in Weisgerber, 268), but Delvaux favors a more surrealist ambiguity or antinomy by blurring the boundary between reality and imagination visually, verbally, and auditorily. The themes of "mad love," journeys into mirror worlds of madness and death,[29] chance encounters (cf. Breton's "objective chance") and the circulation of objects with dissociated names, uses, and meanings, all concur toward a surrealist interpretation of the film.

L'homme au crâne rasé is Delvaux's only black and white feature and he used "a spectrum of greys within the blacks and whites rather than a contrasting chiaroscuro or the violent clashes of colour" (Nysenholc 1994, 171). Such painterly touches express Govert's limbo state, his imperceptible passages from reality into dream / imagination / hallucination and prefigure Delvaux's inclusion of plastic artworks in the next films.

Like his last feature, L'oeuvre au noir (1988), Delvaux's second one, Un soir, un train[30] deals extensively with death. He uses a double struc-

29. Madness evokes Leonora Carrington's autobiographical narrative, Down Below, first published in VVV (New York, 1944), and death points to the Orpheus legend and Cocteau's film Orphée (1950), 1h 52 min. BW, directed by Jean Cocteau, produced by André Paulvé, France, with Jean Marais and Maria Casarès.

30. Un soir, un train / One Evening, a Train . . . (1968), color, 92mn, produced by Parc Film/Fox Europa (Paris and Brussels), script by André Delvaux from the short story "De Trein der Traagheid" by Johan Daisne, with Yves Montand, Anouk Aimée, Adriana Bogdan, Senne Rouffaer.

ture, much like Breton's communicating vessels, with a twice-told story on each side of the mirror of the afterworld. The film begins in black and white, tracking across winter landscapes, to the tune of a sinister song about the fading and freezing of love with the advent of the cold season (Borgomano, 72). The image then takes on drab colors and introduces human presence with close-ups of an old woman's hands holding her son Mathias's, preceding full shots of them both in an old people's home. It is All Saints' Day, the day of the dead, and the mother wants chrysanthemums for her late husband's grave. Delvaux summed up the plot as follows:

> It is a film about death, about a selfish man, about a superb, sublime and silent woman and a journey. The journey means the knowledge of death, it's a film about winter landscapes in Belgium, about people I have known: a university professor etc. But all that is what the film is about, not the film itself. The film itself is the form. (Nysenholc 1994, 99)

The film is in French, with two French stars, Yves Montand as the Belgian linguistics professor with a Flemish name, Mathias Vreeman (bilingual like Delvaux) and Anouk Aimée as his French partner Anne, a stage set and costume designer. The crisis the couple is going through reflects the social unrest and linguistic conflict surrounding them. Various disruptions and encounters with death punctuate the diegesis. Mathias interrupts his class because of a student strike and joins Anne at a rehearsal. The interpolated play is his own version of *Elkerlyk* (Everyman), and the scene shows Everyman confronting Death. The couple go home to a gourmet supper, quarrel over Death's costume and take a tense walk. Anne voices her bitterness over Mathias's refusal to marry her, merely to avoid the embarrassment of a French wife within prejudiced Flemish academe. She then disappears abruptly but later joins Mathias in the train taking him to a Flemish university for a lecture. The other passengers prevent them from communicating. Mathias falls asleep. When he awakes, Anne has vanished again and the train has stopped.

The displacement from a "real" world to a fantastic one and from the first realist part of the film to its specular oneiric double is not immediately obvious. Mathias gets off the train, obsessively looking for Anne, and encounters his former professor, Hernhutter, and one of his students, Val: his past and future selves or doubles. The train leaves without them and they wander through another deserted winter landscape, to a village whose inhabitants' language and behavior remain incomprehensible to them. They see a strange film (cf. the play in part I), people ignore them (cf. the hostile striking students or the strangers in the train), enter an eerie inn, presided over by Moïra (Adriana Bogdan), Death as a young woman (cf. Everyman's Death) and are served a refined meal (cf. Anne and Mathias's supper). People start dancing like robots. Val dances with Moïra and begins to understand her language, to Mathias's dismay. Suddenly a loud train whistle, screeching brakes, and sirens break up the scene. Mathias remains alone with Moïra. The location turns into a train crash site and Moïra becomes a nurse, in whose arms Mathias regains consciousness and learns there has been an accident. He wanders off and discovers Anne and Val among the dead. Mathias clings to his lover's corpse in desperation. The passage through the mirror of death echoes Cocteau's film on the Orpheus myth (see note 29): during the train journey Mathias had looked back at Anne-Eurydice in dream and memory flashbacks, and had realized the vital importance of love too late.[31] His younger self, Val, had substituted Death (Moïra) for Love (Anne). Delvaux compared the uncertain passage from Eros to Thanatos, or conversely from the twilight zone to the train tracks, to Magritte's 1954 uncanny juxtaposition of night and day in *The Empire of Lights* (Nysenholc 1985, 99). Without love there can be no communication and as the film closes, Mathias is left suspended in what Breton calls the "long dominant death-drive brought on by the loss of a lover" (Breton 1937, 47).

Delvaux was about to shoot *Belle*,[32] the only fiction film he wrote entirely himself, when he was asked to adapt a text by Julien Gracq. Although *Rendez-vous à Bray* precedes *Belle,* the latter comes closer in form and content to *L'homme au crâne rasé* and *Un soir, un train,* so I will discuss it first. Like *Un soir, un train, Belle* grew out of the opening pages of Nerval's *Aurélia* and deals with love, death, creativity, and language. The hero and focalizer, Mathieu Grégoire, is a poet. Delvaux uses alternate montage to structure the protagonist's double life (real and imaginary), represented by two women, his wife Jeanne and (prob-

31. Although some surrealists befriended Cocteau, Breton despised him and refused to let him be a member of the group. However, today the links between Cocteau's films and surrealism seem obvious and I would like to contend that the same applies to Delvaux's work.

32. *Belle* (1973), original script by André Delvaux, shot in French, color, 35mm, 93 min.

ably imagined) lover Belle, in two Belgian locations, the small town of Spa and the wild woods and marshes of the Fagne(s), Mathieu's main source of inspiration. This doubling process becomes systematic as the film unfolds. Couples proliferate, especially in the "magic" realm of dream, fantasy and (often jealous) imagination. On the "real" side are Mathieu (Jean-Luc Bideau) and Jeanne (Danièle Delorme), their daughter Marie (Stéphane Excoffier) and her fiancé John (John Dobrynine); on the other side: Mathieu and Belle (Adriana Bogdan), a foreign beauty he meets in the woods; the incestuous couple Mathieu longs to form with Marie; Belle and her compatriot "l'Étranger" (the Foreigner or Stranger)—doubles of Marie and John; and finally Mathieu's friend Victor (René Coggio) and Jeanne, whom the latter fancies.

Delvaux creates parallel patterns in both plots: Mathieu sees drops of blood in the snow after running over an animal in the Fagne and drops of coffee on the kitchen table at home, while discussing Marie's cat with her; later both Belle and Marie ask Mathieu for money. Traveling proves important again. Mathieu's white Volvo creates a link between his two worlds, as he drives it back and forth between his two erotic partners, Jeanne and Belle, just as in *L'homme au crâne rasé* the professor's black vehicle had driven Govert to the conversely morbid autopsy and (supposedly) to Fran's death.

Like Govert and Mathias, Mathieu is weathering a mid-life crisis, privately and professionally. He still loves Jeanne but cannot deal with Marie's imminent wedding, hence his flight to the Fagne and into poetry: the first produces Belle and the second Louise Labé, a French renaissance woman poet, whose erotic verses Mathieu chooses for a public lecture. Mathieu's wild Fagne life soon catches up with his respectable existence in Spa: during his lecture on Labé the camera pans down to the poet's muddy trousers and he savagely punches a spectator, mistaking him for l'Étranger. The incident precipitates legal intervention and Mathieu drives Marcel, the local police officer, to the Fagne after confessing to the murder of l'Étranger, whom he thinks Belle killed. Marcel informs Mathieu of the existence of some smugglers from across the German border (Belle and l'Étranger?). The police then drain a pond known as "Le trou noir" (The Black Hole) (significantly under a bridge), where Mathieu and Belle had allegedly thrown the body and only find a dead dog. Mathieu's Fagne adventure has come full circle, having begun with his car's hitting Belle's dog and her shooting it. L'étranger, with his long hair and shaggy coat, could have been a hallucination at the sight of the animal (Joseph Marty suggests a connection with *Beauty and the Beast* [99]). Belle and her dog are also a transposition of Marie and her cat. Once again, Delvaux preserves the ambiguity.

Free from adaptation, Delvaux clearly exposed his own magic realist pattern in *Belle*. Until *Femme entre chien et loup* (1979) and *Benvenuta* (1983), which have women as focalizers, Delvaux's subjects were all men, whose female objects of desire remain fascinating enigmas and poetic muses like the surrealists' "femmes-sphinx"[33]: Fran, Anne, Belle, and "Elle" in *Rendez-vous à Bray*. In the latter film and *Belle*, they are doubled and mirrored by fetishized paintings. In *Belle*, Mathieu and Victor are mesmerized by a picture in the museum library of a woman, naked under an open blue kimono, her genitals exposed. The camera at one point zooms in on the middle of her body, cutting off the head, like a Freudian *Witz* referring to Max Ernst's *La femme sans/cent Tête(s)*[34] and highlighting the two men's sexual obsessions. Later Marie wears the same robe in a dream of Mathieu's and the color blue suffuses the Spa sequences (as in parts of *Un soir, un train*), while browns set the tone in the Fagne. Mathieu's long erotic dream includes a significant sequence emulating the surrealist painter Paul Delvaux's sensual twilight settings: Marie and Mathieu are seen from behind walking along the Spa train-station platform, she naked and he fully clothed, in the Magrittian glow of a red lantern. A fantasy of Breton's in *Nadja* comes to mind and links the dream of Marie with the vision of Belle: "I have always longed to meet a beautiful naked woman at night in a wood."[35]

*Rendez-vous à Bray*,[36] a Franco-Belgian production, shot in French, is Delvaux's most romantic and aesthetic film, and the only one adapted from a non-Belgian text, by the French surrealist Julien Gracq.[37] Here Delvaux superimposes his individual, strictly structured magic realism onto Gracq's equally personal, almost baroque surrealism. The film consequently both resembles and remains distinct from the other three. The unique male point of view is conveyed by a

33. See Sarane Alexandrian, *Les libérateurs de l'amour* (Paris: Seuil, 1977), 238–39, regarding Gustave Moreau and sphinx-like women.

34. The title of Ernst's collage novel, *La femme 100 têtes*, (Paris: Carrefour, 1929), creates a pun combining "headless woman" (sans tête) and "woman with 100 heads" (cent têtes).

35. André Breton, *Nadja* (1928) (Paris: Gallimard, Folio, 1998), 40.

36. *Rendez-vous à Bray* (1971), color, 35mm, 93mn.

37. The short story "Le Roi Cophetua," in Julien Gracq's *La presqu'île* (Paris: José Corti, 1970), 183–251.

younger, unattached subject. Delvaux names Gracq's anonymous narrator/protagonist Julien Eschenbach, condensing Stendhal's romantic hero Julien Sorel[38] with a medieval German poet, Wolfram von Eschenbach (1170–1220) who, like Julien, bore his poverty with great dignity. The film unfolds during World War I. Laure Borgomano identifies its atmosphere as Proustian (41), for like the author of *La recherche*, Delvaux uses time as a theme as well as a formal element. The filmmaker reads Gracq's story as follows: "Nothing could be simpler than a man who, having been invited by a friend (Jacques Nueil) to join him in the country during the war, goes and waits for him there and finds a young woman; the friend never turns up and he leaves the next morning at dawn" (Nysenholc 1985, 100). The film maintains Gracq's idea of a parenthesis in time and space, and Julien embarks on a long poetic meditation inspired by the penumbra of an old house on All Saints' Day (cf. *Un soir, un train*), the works of art surrounding him, his memories of Nueil and the bewitching young woman who, like Belle, appears out of nowhere. Distant drums and canons recall the war and Delvaux creates a period piece effect by using archaic irises as punctuation instead of his usual fade-outs.

Flashbacks occur not only during Julien's short train journey, as in Mathias's in *Un soir, un train*, but also while he waits for Nueil at La Fougeraie. Delvaux devises various levels of doubling, between past and present, war and peace, Julien's solitude and the joyful prewar company of Nueil and the latter's fiancée Odile. Later, real and imagined couples are confronted, as in *Belle*: Nueil and Odile (real) with Julien and Odile (Nueil's fantasy) in the past; in the present (in Julien's imagination) Nueil and Elle, the nameless woman at La Fougeraie, with Julien and Elle that night (real). As always, Delvaux increases the impression of strangeness with an international cast. The German actor Mathieu Carrière, then only twenty-one, plays a proud, romantic Julien, robbed of his innocence by a tantalizingly reserved and more mature Elle, the Danish Anna Karina, Godard's fetish actress of the 60s. The bubbly French Bulle Ogier and more mephistophelian Belgian Roger Van Hool as Odile and Jacques embody their opposites. Delvaux's Jacques and Julien pay tribute to Truffaut's *Jules et Jim* (1961) and a sequence of the threesome watching a Fantômas film emulates the young surrealists.

Here, too, form and meaning overlap. Music structures the story.

---

38. In his most famous novel, *Le rouge et le noir* (1830).

Julien was a pianist before the war and Jacques a composer. Flashbacks show them practicing and an unfinished nocturne by Jacques awaits Julien on the piano at La Fougeraie. Like the three previous features, *Rendez-vous à Bray* begins with a song, an odd child's nursery rhyme about the death of a bird, sung by a little girl under Julien's window in Paris to a tune by Brahms. Julien later hums it or plays it on the piano. Furthermore, Delvaux explains how he based the film's "completely abstract structure" (Nysenholc 1985; 107) on the rondo form, by using alternate montage between past and present scenes; according to Laure Borgomano: "the present increasingly becomes a mirror for the past" (51). External time echoes and merges with the internal dimension Deleuze calls *"nappes de temps"*[39] (sheets of time), as Julien becomes aware that his stay at La Fougeraie has probably been programmed by Jacques, as a rerun of their past together: the welcome, their favorite foods and wines, the music, the consenting woman (Jacques had formerly attempted to organize Julien's sexual initiation by Odile, a scheme that works with Elle).

Recurring objects are photographs of the three friends, confronting past and present, and specular paintings, as in *Belle*. Gracq's title, "Le Roi Cophetua," is echoed by his narrator's quoting from Shakespeare's *Romeo and Juliet* (II:i): "When King Cophetua loved the beggar maid," while contemplating a painting at La Fougeraie, with no mention of the artist. Delvaux shows what is unmistakably Burne-Jones's *King Cophetua and the Beggar Maid*,[40] and recreates the configuration of the young king at the poor girl's feet with Julien and Elle. Twelve years later he restages the scene in *Benvenuta*,[41] using metatextual characters: the novelist Jeanne (Françoise Fabian), with the filmmaker François (Mathieu Carrière again, by then a favorite actor of Delvaux's) kneeling before her. The musical, temporal, and spatial rondo also applies to art and life, inter- and intratextuality, and the repetitive connections between the first four features, extending to *Benvenuta*. The most important link among these works is the music by Delvaux's staunchest collaborator, Frédéric Devreese. The latter's soundtracks highlight the ominous presence of death, emanating in *Rendez-vous à*

---

39. See Gilles Deleuze, *L'image-temps* (Paris: Éditions de Minuit, 1985).

40. Sir Edward Burne-Jones, *King Cophetua and the Beggar Maid* (1884), oil on canvas, 290 × 136 cm, London, Tate Britain.

41. André Delvaux, *Benvenuta* (1983, Belgium, France, Italy) adapted from Suzanne Lilar's novel *La confession anonyme* (1960), 105 min., with Fanny Ardant, Victoria Gassman, Françoise Fabian, Mathieu Carrière.

*Bray* from the peace-time flashbacks and the hypothetically testamentary quality of Jacques Nueil's invitation.

To conclude, in Delvaux's early fiction features, surrealism and magic realism dance a *pas de deux*, with the *danse macabre* as a negative mirror, traversed by an Orphean quest for love. Magic-realist doubles and surrealist antinomies prove to be closely related, though the first are deliberately constructed and the second more dependent on chance and automatism. The strong influence and heredity of Belgian surrealist painting make Delvaux's films visually surrealist and reinforce surrealist themes like mad love and desire, insanity, dreams, rêverie, Freudian fetishism (as in the frequent close-ups of hands), objects out of context, poetry as a way of life, mysterious and magical women, uncanny landscapes, and so on. Delvaux's magic realism was self-proclaimed and the fundamental expression of his "Belgitude," but strayed far afield from Daisne's more rigid and moral stance; his surrealist tendencies owe more to Magritte, Paul Delvaux, and Gracq than to Breton or even Buñuel. Furthermore, as a marginal, minor medium for both surrealism and magic realism, film allowed Delvaux more freedom and interdisciplinary scope with which to transcend the differences.

Finally, it is a pleasure to be able to announce that at long last the Belgian Cultural Services are aiding scholars to gain access to Delvaux's first four feature films. The Wallon community has recently [January 2005] produced a DVD of *Rendez-vous à Bray* including with it two of Delvaux's short films [*Met Dieric Bouts/Avec Dieric Bouts* (1975) and *1001 Films* (1989)], and Gracq's short story in booklet form. A second DVD of *De man die zijn haar kort liet knippen / L'Homme au crâne rasé* has just been commercialized [March 2005] by the Flemish community, in Daisne's original language. They should both be distributed outside Belgium within the next few months and it is to be hoped that DVD's of *Belle* and *Un soir, un train* will follow.

KATHARINE CONLEY

# Surrealism and Outsider Art: From the "Automatic Message" to André Breton's Collection

From the beginning of the surrealist movement, André Breton pondered the relationship between surrealism and what became known as *art brut* after the invention of the term by Jean Dubuffet in 1945, rendered into English as *outsider art* by Roger Cardinal in 1972.[1] Breton did so most pointedly in "The Automatic Message" (1933) where he most clearly distinguishes between surrealist and mediumistic automatism. With his illustrations, however, as Cardinal has pointed out, Breton tells a different story.[2] These were all examples of what would later be called outsider art: drawings by visionaries, the mentally ill (including one by Nadja), and mediums, in particular a drawing by Mme. Fondrillon already used by Breton in 1925 as the frontispiece to the editorial from *La révolution surréaliste* in which he proclaimed the existence of surrealist art (Figure 1).[3] Breton implies with this drawing that mediumism and surrealism might actually be very similar. Here I will examine some of the terms Breton uses in "The Automatic Message" to compare Bretonian surrealist automatism, inspired by Sigmund Freud, with the popular spiritist automatism so in vogue in France starting in the nineteenth century, in order to understand better the relation between the two, particularly with regard to Breton's private collection.

1. Roger Cardinal, *Outsider Art* (New York: Praeger Publishers, 1972). He updates the term in "Marginalia," *Marginalia: Perspectives on Outsider Art*, ed. Ans van Berkum, Roger Cardinal, Jos ten Berge, Colin Rhodes (Zwolle: De Stadshof Museum, 2000), 51–75.
2. Cardinal, "André Breton and the Automatic Message," *André Breton*, ed. Ramona Fotiade (Exeter: Elm Bank Publications, 2000), 23–36.
3. With this proclamation Breton took over the journal in response to the questioning of the possibility of surrealist painting by Pierre Naville and Max Morise.

**YFS 109,** *Surrealism and Its Others,* ed. Katharine Conley and Pierre Taminiaux,
© 2006 by Yale University.

DESSIN AUTOMATIQUE, PAR M^me FONDRILLON, AGÉE DE 79 ANS.
*(La Révolution surréaliste, 1925)*

*Figure 1.* Automatic Drawing by Mme Fondrillon, 79 years of age.
Reproduced in *La révolution surréaliste* 1.4 (1925) and "The Automatic
Message" in *Minotaure* 3–4 (1933).

In the *Manifesto of Surrealism* from 1924, Breton equates surrealism with automatism, defining the word *surrealism* as "psychic automatism in its pure state" based on the "actual functioning of
thought . . . in the absence of any control exercised by reason," an as-
sertion he confirms nine years later in "The Automatic Message," and
again in 1938 and 1941 (26).[4] For automatism to be expressed, however,
some degree of mediation must be involved, most often in the form of
a body—which can be one's own—suddenly speaking in an unfamiliar
voice, and enacting Arthur Rimbaud's formula for the experience of

4. See André Breton and Paul Eluard, *Dictionnaire abrégé du surréalisme* (Paris: José
Corti, 1991 [1938]), 4; and Breton, "Artistic Genesis and Perspective of Surrealism," *Surrealism and Painting,* trans. Simon Watson Taylor (Boston: MFA Publications, 2002
[1965]), 68.

otherness within the self, "*Je* est *un autre.*" In addition, an element of clear-headed rationality is needed to witness the experience, as Breton suggests in the *Manifesto* with the image of strong currents in a body of water: "If the depths of our mind contain within it strange forces capable of augmenting those on the surface, or of waging a victorious battle against them, there is every reason to seize them—first to seize them, then, if need be, to submit them to the control of our reason."[5] *Surreality* for him is "the future resolution of these two states, dream and reality, which are seemingly so contradictory, into a kind of absolute reality" (14).

Surrealist automatic practice requires both the conscious and unconscious minds to work in concert, in other words, leading Breton, in "The Automatic Message," to argue that surrealist automatism plays a unifying role: "contrary to what spiritualism aims to do—dissociate the psychological personality from the medium—Surrealism proposes nothing less than to unify that personality. It is obvious that, for us, the question of the exteriority of . . . one's 'voice' could not be posed" (137).[6] Whereas mediums "set down letters or lines in strictly *mechanical* fashion," surrealists seek a conscious receptivity, a willed passivity (132).[7] The surrealist interprets such inner voices as manifestations of the unconscious mind, unlike the often less educated medium who believes that these voices come from outside—from other people, beyond the grave, even other planets.

And yet Breton situated his first explanation of the new term surrealism as "a certain psychic automatism" in an essay from 1922 entitled "The Mediums Enter,"[8] written during the group's initial phase of experimentation with hypnotic trances, of which Robert Desnos was the undisputed star. As a result, two years later in the *Manifesto* it was Desnos who, for Breton, came the "closest to the Surrealist truth" (29). Desnos was thus something of a medium for Breton and his drawings were linked in the *Manifesto* to the art of the mentally ill, associating him with two of the "three broad types" of artist outsiders originally

5. Breton, "Manifesto of Surrealism (1924)," *Manifestoes of Surrealism*, trans. Richard Seaver and Helen R. Lane (Ann Arbor, MI: University of Michigan Press, 1972), 10.

6. In the *Manifesto* Breton claims that only true surrealists have *"heard the Surrealist voice"* (27).

7. Marguerite Bonnet, "Le message automatique: Notice," Breton, *Oeuvres complètes*, vol. 2 (Paris: Gallimard, 1992), 1528, my translation.

8. Breton, "The Mediums Enter," *The Lost Steps*, trans. Mark Polizzotti (Lincoln, NE: University of Nebraska Press, 1996 [1924]), 90.

specified by Cardinal in *Outsider Art*: "schizophrenics, mediums and innocents" (35). In reference to these drawings, Breton introduces the possibility of surrealist automatic art for the first time, having just expressed admiration for the "insane" and compared their innocence to his own: "These people are honest to a fault, and their naiveté has no peer but my own" (5). After he explains hearing his first automatic phrase—a striking image of divided consciousness, "'There is a man cut in two by the window'"—Breton adds a footnote about drawings made by Desnos in imitation of the drawings of the mentally ill, which Breton takes as "proof" that automatism can be visually, as well as verbally, expressed (21). Thus the first reference to visual surrealism coincided with its similarity to the art of the mentally ill, particularly in reference to the sort of drawing André Masson would publish in *La révolution surréaliste*—the sort of drawing that, like writing but unlike painting, allows the pen or pencil to move freely, spontaneously.

Later, in a number of *Le surréalisme au service de la révolution* from 1931, Max Ernst's *Oedipus*, created in homage to the schizophrenic August Natterer's *Miraculous Shepherd*, was published as surrealist art.[9] Natterer had been a patient of Hans Prinzhorn, the psychiatrist who collected his patients's work and whose collection influenced Dubuffet. Prinzhorn's book, *The Artistry of the Mentally Ill*, introduced this art to many Europeans including Ernst and the surrealists.[10] Like Prinzhorn's, the surrealist's eyes were trained according to a modernist, primitivist aesthetic that attracted them to some works more than others (a situation some critics of Prinzhorn argue led the artist-patients themselves to produce art that would please him, since culture is difficult to escape completely, even for the mentally ill).[11] In *Primitivism and Modernism*, Colin Rhodes explains that while "European beliefs placed the savage in Central and Southern Africa, the Americas and Oceania . . . the West itself has long believed that it contains its own primitives—peasant populations, children and the insane."[12] The sur-

---

9. See John MacGregor, *The Discovery of the Art of the Insane* (Princeton: Princeton University Press, 1989), 279–80.

10. Sarah Wilson, "From the Asylum to the Museum," *Parallel Visions*, ed. Maurice Tuchman and Carol Eliel (Princeton: Princeton UP-LACMA, 1993), 144, n. 7.

11. See Bettina Brand-Claussen, "The Collection of Works of Art in the Psychiatric Clinic, Heidelberg," *Beyond Reason* (London: Hayward Gallery, 1996), 13; and Cardinal's "Marginalia" (note 1).

12. Colin Rhodes, *Primitivism and Modern Art* (London: Thames and Hudson, 1994), 7.

realist's taste was shaped by the culture of their time, by a primitivist inclination to admire simplicity.

Breton and the surrealists had a tendency to mix up surrealist, mediumistic, visionary, and psychotic art from the start, even if the mentally ill actually share little in common with school teachers who practice mediumism in their spare time, postmen who construct visionary buildings on weekends, or surrealists steeped in avant-garde intellectual life (see Cardinal, note 2). In the inaugural issue of *La révolution surréaliste,* despite arguing against the possibility of surrealist painting because of the fundamentally unautomatic nature of its process, Max Morise implicitly compares these groups when he writes: "Let us admire madmen and mediums who manage to fix their most fugitive visions, as does, in a different way, the man devoted to surrealism."[13] In the special issue of *Variétés* that took the measure of surrealist activity in 1929 immediately preceding the *Second Manifesto,* Breton and the surrealists included illustrations by Hélène Smith, whose voices often came from Mars, and the visionary postman Ferdinand Cheval, who built a fantastic *Ideal Palace* in his backyard with stones and pebbles picked up on his daily rounds. These images, side by side with photographs of British Columbian native art and works by Joan Miró, Yves Tanguy, and Georges Malkine, stand together as though in a private collection, composed, as Naomi Schor affirms about collections, "of objects wrenched out of their contexts of origin and reconfigured into the self-contained, self-referential context of the collection itself."[14] And in the number of *Cahiers d'art* that served as the catalogue for the surrealist exhibition of objects at the Charles Ratton Gallery in 1936,[15] a comparable collection of images again speaks in the visual language of surrealist images, which operate according to "the fortuitous juxtaposition" of *"two more or less distant realities,"* like the "chance encounter on an operating table of a sewing machine and an umbrella" from Isidore Ducasse's legendary aphorism, in order to produce a revelatory "spark," a "luminous phenomenon" (*Manifesto,* 20, 37).

After World War Two surrealism was so well established that Breton had lost the need to insist so much on the differences between his

13. Max Morise, "Les yeux enchantés," *La révolution surréaliste* 1/1 (1924), 16.

14. Naomi Schor, "Collecting Paris," *Cultures of Collecting,* ed. John Elsner and Roger Cardinal (Melbourne: Melbourne University Press, 1994), 256.

15. Breton, "La crise de l'objet," *Cahiers d'art* 11/6–10 (1936): 22.

intellectual movement and populist spiritism with its partiality for the overtly supernatural. A surrealist journal was even entitled *Médium* in the 1950s and Breton wrote a book on *L'art magique*. In a series of essays from the 1940s and 1950s written after he collaborated with Dubuffet and the gallery owner Ratton on the creation of the Compagnie de l'Art Brut in 1948, Breton persisted in grouping the artwork of mediums, visionaries, and the mentally ill together, according to Dubuffet's definition for *art brut* artists as "persons unscathed by artistic culture."[16] Perhaps he did so partly *because* so little surrealist painting convincingly approximated automatist practice; it was with artists like these outsiders that Breton could share his faith in automatism, that he could pursue the dream of what Elza Adamowicz critically calls his "totalizing project of intercultural analogies" (my translation).[17]

In "Joseph Crépin," Breton conflates the work of Crépin, discovered at an *art brut* exhibition in 1948, with that of four mediums and visionaries: Victorien Sardou, whose *House of Mozart on the Planet Jupiter* served as a frontispiece for "The Automatic Message," Leon Petitjean, portraitist of spirits, Augustin Lesage, who believed his hand was guided by Leonardo da Vinci,[18] and the postman Cheval.[19] He reserves particular praise for the "admirable Adolf Wölfli," the Swiss mental patient whose work he, Dubuffet, and Prinzhorn collected. For Breton, all these artists have "affinities"; their work shares "a special hypnotic virtue" in an echo of the hypnotic trances practiced by the surrealists themselves in the 1920s (307). He published these essays in his definitive edition of *Surrealism and Painting* from 1965, alongside his essays on Pablo Picasso, Marcel Duchamp, Joan Miró, Yves Tanguy, and others, showing that these artists belonged together unproblematically for him, according to his desire to globalize culture from within.

Breton's most impassioned defense of the art of the mentally ill, "The Art of the Insane," was illustrated with works by the mental patient Aloïse Corbaz (collected by Prinzhorn, Dubuffet, and Breton).[20] He concludes with the following resounding endorsement: "Through

16. Jean Dubuffet, "Art Brut in Preference to the Cultural Arts," *Art Brut: Madness and Marginalia, Art & Text* 27 (1988): 33.

17. Elza Adamowicz, *Ceci n'est pas un tableau, les écrits surréalistes sur l'art* (Paris: L'âge d'homme, 2004), 127.

18. John Beardsley and Roger Cardinal, *Private Worlds: Classic Outsider Art from Europe* (Katonah, NY: Katonah Museum of Art, 1999), 22.

19. Breton, "Joseph Crépin," *Surrealism and Painting*, 298–307.

20. Breton, "The Art of the Insane: Freedom to Roam Abroad," *Surrealism and Painting*, 313–17.

an astonishing dialectical effect, the factors of close confinement and the renunciation of all worldly vanities . . . together provide the guarantees of a total authenticity which is sadly lacking everywhere else" (316). In this essay Breton adds the group of so-called "primitive peoples" to the mentally ill, mediums, visionaries and surrealists, claiming that they, too, share a commitment to authenticity (315). For Breton, in an echo of his definition of surrealist automatism, the art of the insane, like that of primitive peoples, is "never constrained, or smothered, by 'reasonable' objectives." The outsider artist Scottie Wilson, whose work Breton collected, describes his own process as similarly unconstrained in Cardinal's *Outsider Art*: "It's a feeling, you can *not* explain. You're born with it, and it just comes out. That's *you*, and that's all about it" (54).

The mediating terms used by Breton to describe automatic experience between 1922 and 1965—honesty, naiveté, truth, freedom, authenticity, and the notion of the primitive—all refer back to the *purity* he seeks from psychic automatism. They recall Dubuffet's notion that outsider artists are *unscathed* by culture, as well as the desire Breton articulates in the *Manifesto* to rediscover the sense of wonder linked to childhood. Through surrealism he advocates relocating "a sentiment of being unintegrated" into civilized culture, a return to the "real life" to which one is closest in childhood before *"having gone astray"* (40). He evidently seeks terms for automatism that convey its virtue of being as unmediated by Western high culture as possible. The idea of digging into the psyche in order to find a more unadulterated self conforms to one of two definitions for the French adjective *primitif* from the *Petit Robert* dictionary: 1) that which is at the source, the origin, a vertical relation, one of depth; and 2) that which is the first or oldest, a horizontal relation connected to time. This double meaning may be found in Freud's comparison, in *Totem and Taboo*, of "primitive peoples" with both "prehistoric man" and modern "neurotics," suggesting that within every twentieth-century human traces of a distant past coexist with a present "system of thought" that still sees magic in things.[21] In "The Automatic Message" what may be found buried in the psyche is literally a treasure crystallized by time. Automatism re-

21. Sigmund Freud, *Totem and Taboo*, ed. and trans. James Strachey (New York: W. W. Norton, 1950 [1913]), 75. The notion that so-called primitive peoples lived in ahistorical time was quite common at the turn of the last century. See Johannes Fabian, *Time and the Other* (New York: Columbia University Press, 1983).

sponds to the need to "draw blindly from our subjective treasure for the unique temptation of throwing here and there onto the sand a handful of foamy seaweed together with emeralds" (376).

The word *primitive* also plays a role also in "The Automatic Message" through Breton's suggestion that automatism is at its best in its primitive state. In the context of a lament that surrealist automatism can often yield disappointing results, Breton regrets "the obstacles which . . . succeed in turning away the verbal flow from its primitive direction" (130–31, translation modified). *Primitive* here clearly takes on a positive aspect according to the adjective's first definition in the sense of an unobstructed access to an original source. Similarly, in describing how mediums have often encountered comparable obstacles, he uses the word *primitive* to propose that, through an overly facile practice of mediumistic hence dissociative automatism, a school principal, Miss X, came to regret her lost "primitive automatism" (137, translation modified). Automatism, a process that takes one *down* into the psyche, for Breton also constitutes a way *back*, as though in time, to a *unique, original faculty* to which easy access has been lost, except for those Western primitives considered to be outside culture. In his conclusion Breton suggests that everyone could potentially unify her or his own personality through automatism if it were possible to counteract "the dissociation of a *unique, original faculty*" promoted by Western culture. Such a dissociation has been successfully resisted, in his view, only by "primitive peoples and children" (143, translation modified).

Breton's evocation of primitive peoples in "The Automatic Message" echoes the surrealists' primitivist sensibilities and their heightened awareness in the 1930s of so-called primitive art as evidenced by the anticolonial exhibition they mounted in opposition to the official Colonial Exhibition held in Paris from May to November of 1931. This counter-exhibition grouped African, Oceanic, and Native American objects with what appears to be, in a photograph published in *Le surréalisme au service de la révolution*, at least one Christian statuette in a group labeled "European Fetishes."[22] This grouping and the use of the word "fetish" conforms to the etymological sense of the fetish as an ob-

22. Steven Harris identifies one of the European fetishes as a Catholic Madonna and child and the central figure as an African statue of a Europeanized person of the sort deemed unauthentic by the organizers of the Colonialist Exhibition. See *Surrealist Art and Thought in the 1930s* (Cambridge: Cambridge University Press, 2004), 53; 70–71.

ject produced and named through an encounter between radically different social cultures. In the Renaissance, as William Pietz explains, Portuguese traders used the word to describe African amulets and the unfamiliar and suspicious religious practices attached to them, just as Dutch Protestants later used the word to describe Catholic religious objects in much the same way.[23] This juxtaposition seems to ask: Whose beliefs linked to things are more effective than others? Such a leveling idealism was also reflected in the sign the surrealists made of Marx's motto "A people who oppresses others knows not how to be free" (my translation). They were fascinated with the capacity of objects to retain an uncanny presence, almost to communicate, and at times to release psychic secrets. Beyond their appreciation of a primitivist aesthetic, the surrealists sought to access a sense of the primitive within—within things, and within themselves.

The surrealists also actively sought what Pietz calls "cross-cultural situations" productive of fetish objects (7), particularly through their practice of turning objects away from their original function, as with Duchamp's readymades, such as *Fountain*. Johanna Malt has persuasively argued that the surrealist object was unique in its multivalent incorporation of both the Freudian sexual notion of the fetish and the Marxist idea of the commodity fetish while maintaining a canny "awareness of its own fetish status."[24] The surrealists believed in remaining ever receptive to the sorts of chance events that bring insight, often in the form of an accidental encounter with a place, a person, or a thing. The publication of "The Automatic Message" coincided with an understanding of objects in the 1930s as another form of mediation, almost a language, between the conscious self and the unconscious mind, like the speaking poet's body or the artist's pen.[25] Objects can provoke insight in the viewer according to the same magical operation

23. William Pietz, "The Problem of the Fetish, I," *Res* 9 (1985): 7. Rey Chow's suggestion that Marx's ambiguous view of the fetish, which has given rise "to a prevalent modernist tendency to regard things as superficial and morally suspect," may have its origin in this understanding of the fetish as belonging always to the *wrong* religion. See "Fateful Attachments," *Critical Inquiry: Things* 28/1 (Autumn 2001): 288–89.

24. Johanna Malt, *Obscure Objects of Desire: Surrealism, Fetishism, and Politics* (Oxford: Oxford University Press, 2004), 101; 108.

25. In 1935 he stated that "it is on the *object* that the most lucid eyes in surrealism have been focused lately," in "Situation surréaliste de l'objet," *Oeuvres complètes*, vol. 2, 474, my translation. See also Phil Powrie, "The Surrealist *Poème-Objet*," *Surrealism: Surrealist Visuality*, ed. Silvano Levy (New York: New York University Press, 1997), 57–77.

of chance as the automatic gestures that created them. It was in *Nadja* that Breton first described discovering an object at a flea market. He found it by chance, which, as he explains, had the force to admit him "to an almost forbidden world of sudden parallels, petrifying coincidences . . . of harmonies struck as though on the piano, flashes of light that would make you see, really *see.*"[26] Starting in 1931 with the third number of *Le surréalisme au service de la révoluion,* Breton and Salvidor Dali raised the question of the surrealist object in a series of essays, and in two exhibitions at the Pierre Colle and Ratton galleries in 1933 and 1936. For Breton in 1934 the object "alone" could help the one who finds or makes it "recognize the marvelous precipitate of desire. It alone can enlarge the universe, causing it to relinquish some of its opacity."[27] Breton repeats this link to desire in 1937, declaring that objects could "help reveal to each individual his own desire. . . . Just as poetry must be made by all, so those objects must be of use to all."[28]

Surrealist objects, assembled like collages and glued together in shapes and boxes, or found and renamed, had a psychoanalytic rather than an aesthetic function. Anyone could make them just like anyone could hear the "subliminal message" of surrealist automatism, as Breton explains in "The Automatic Message": "Surrealism's distinctive feature is to have proclaimed the total equality of all normal human beings before the subliminal message" (138). He continues in language that renders the luminosity from the surrealist image in *Manifesto* revelatory, stating that "every man and every woman" has the ability "to tap into this language at will, which has nothing supernatural about it and which, for each and every one of us, is *the* vehicle of revelation" (138). Objects found and made form another essential link between the surrealists and the sorts of self-taught artists who became known as outsider artists, who, in addition to drawing and painting, make objects out of detritus, transforming inanimate everyday things like bits of wood, shells, string, discarded cigarette boxes, pins, and newspapers into haunting figurines evocative of intensely "private worlds" (see note 17), not unlike the "Involuntary Sculptures" published by Brassaï

26. Breton, *Nadja,* trans. Richard Howard (New York: Grove Press, 1960 [1928]), 19.

27. André Breton, *Mad Love,* trans. Mary Ann Caws (Lincoln, NE: University of Nebraska Press, 1987 [1937]), 13–15. Originally published in *Minotaure* 5 (1934): 8–16, as "La beauté sera convulsive."

28. Breton, "Gradiva," *Free Rein,* trans. Michel Parmentier and Jacqueline d'Amboise (Lincoln, NE: University of Nebraska Press, 1995 [1954]), 20.

in the same issue of *Minotaure* as "The Automatic Message"—magnified photographs of toothpaste, soap, and bus tickets.[29]

Outsider objects visible in Cardinal's *Outsider Art* like Pascal Maisonneuve's shell-face sculptures (collected by Breton), Karl Brendel's carvings, or Gaston Chiassac's assemblages, seem at times ghostly, having an unsettling presence (72–73; 158–60, 126–27). Breton would identify such presence as *"latent possibilities"* in reference to surrealist objects in "The Crisis of the Object," from the issue of *Cahiers d'art* that served as a catalogue to the 1936 exhibition, wherein often ordinary objects were transformed into art (22). These *latent possibilities* could be seen as a corollary to Walter Benjamin's notion of aura—of the "cult value" of art objects, particularly those made by hand that, in prehistoric times, had originated as instruments of "magic"—which Benjamin believed got lost through exhibition and reproduction.[30] Malt argues with Theodor Adorno against Benjamin, however, that the magical element at the root of art in general—including those postindustrial works that Benjamin suggests have lost their cult value, and surrealist objects—cannot be denied (58; 108). I would add that the obvious handling involved in turning postindustrial objects away from their original function and renaming them, as with Duchamp's readymades, also serves to reinvest them with cult value, as does their positioning within a private collection, even if this reinvestment is self-conscious and if the cult value functions primarily for the collector. I would also take Malt's comparison of the 1936 exhibition to a "collection of curios" a step further to suggest that the journal number itself emulates a private collection, juxtaposing reproductions of surrealist sculptures, paintings, collages, and exquisite corpse drawings, with objects like Meret Oppenheim's fur-lined teacup, photographs of Cheval's *Palace*, masks and statues from Africa, Oceania, and North America, and an object made by a mentally ill person—one of two Breton acquired in 1929, which had both been published previously (Malt, 132).[31]

The surrealist object was first evoked in the same year as the first *Manifesto* with Breton's call for creating and circulating objects found

29. See my "Modernist Primitivism in 1933: Brassaï's "Involuntary Sculptures" in *Minotaure*," *Modernism/Modernity* 10/1 (January 2003): 127–40.

30. Walter Benjamin, "The Work of Art in the Age of Mechanical Reproduction," *Illuminations*, trans. Harry Zohn (New York: Schocken Books, 1969), 224–25.

31. See *La révolution surréaliste* 5/12 (1929): 42–43; and *Cahiers d'Art* 11/6–7; 8–10 (1936): 50. See also Cardinal, "Surrealism and the Paradigm of the Creative Subject," *Parallel Visions*, 100.

in dreams.[32] Most of the objects made by Breton himself incorporated his handwritten words and fell into the category of the *Poème-objet*. Objects such as the box by a mentally ill person had always illustrated *La révolution surréaliste*, including those made by the surrealists themselves, like Man Ray's humorous *Enigma of Isidore Ducasse*—a sewing machine wrapped in burlap and string. Surrealist objects joined African, Oceanic, and Native American art in surrealist studios, as well, in collections that, while retaining an intensely personal and private character, helped to define the movement's global aesthetic. Like the objects described by Benjamin in "Unpacking My Library," they had almost a conjuring capability, facilitating their collectors's journeys into their own psyches and as though back in time, in an oscillation parallel to the fluctuations of the word *primitive*. As the collector handles his objects, writes Benjamin, "he seems to be seeing through them into their distant past as though inspired."[33] Such a process follows Freud's method of collecting "the trivial detail of the life of everyday objects" in his patient's dreams, proposes John Forrester, which transforms ordinary things into "veritable philosopher's stones."[34]

Picasso, whose work dominated the first installment of Breton's essay "Surrealism and Painting" (from the same number of *La révolution surréaliste* as Mme. Fondrillon's mediumistic drawing), also had an impressive collection of objects in his studio. In a 1923 interview with Florent Fels he claimed that "the African sculptures that hang around almost everywhere in my studios are more witnesses than models."[35] The idea of the object as a witness, as almost a sort of being from the past, was shared by the surrealists partly through their knowledge of the work of the sociologist Marcel Mauss and the art historian Carl Einstein on Oceanic and African religious life and art (Rhodes, 117). Citing Einstein's *African Sculpture* from 1915, Rhodes argues that African sculptures function "as things in themselves: 'The art object is real because it is closed form. Since it is self-contained and extremely powerful, the sense of distance between it and the viewer will necessarily produce an art of enormous intensity'" (117). In the surrealist object this

32. Breton, "Introduction to the Discourse on the Paucity of Reality," *Break of Day*, 16.

33. Benjamin, "Unpacking My Library," *Illuminations*, 61.

34. John Forrester, "Freud and Collecting," *Cultures of Collecting*, 240–41.

35. In William Rubin, "Picasso," *"Primitivism" in 20th-Century Art*, vol. 1, ed. William Rubin (New York: Museum of Modern Art, 1984), 260, 336, n. 64–65.

intensity takes the form of an uncanny semblance of consciousness because of the way it reflects back, to the one who finds or makes it, otherwise hidden aspects of the self as a possible answer to the quintessential question from the opening of Breton's *Nadja*: "Who am I?" (11). James Clifford's identification of the desire to collect objects as essential to "Western identify formation" seems to confirm this.[36] Clifford cites Baudrillard's contention that collecting and creating an "'environment of private objects and their possession . . . is a dimension of our life that is both essential and imaginary. As essential as dreams'" (in Clifford, 220). Through the object, the other within me, from Rimbaud's phrase, is made visible and becomes negotiable.

At the same time, Breton always reserved the right to judge an object's authenticity in the same way he judged automatic writing and art. He was the one, after all, who wrote the unofficial history of surrealism in his manifestoes and essays. He even dictated what the group should or should not read in a list on the back of a surrealist book catalogue from José Corti: Sade, Marx, Baudelaire, and Freud could be read; Plato, Voltaire, Balzac, and Kipling should not. While desiring to match what he idealistically believed to be the *unscathed* honesty of all those residing *outside* mainstream culture, Breton nevertheless remained a consummate insider. Although he may have desired strongly to be *witnessed* by the objects he found and made, he also claimed the right to be the ultimate arbiter of those encounters. He was fascinated by those whose automatic abilities were unrestrained like Nadja and Desnos, but ultimately he distanced himself from them and others whose lack of "common sense" alarmed him in the long run.[37] His own elegant writing consistently cultivated balance, a synthesis of the contradictory forces of reality and dream whose encounter he sought to marshal and document.

Where Breton was most free in his own automatic expression may well have been with his collection, which was dispersed only in 2003 after no single museum would agree to acquire it in its ecclectic entirety.[38] Even if the surrealists moved away from objects after the 1930s (Harris, 229), Breton continued to collect avidly. More than anything he wrote, his collection's juxtapositions and recontextualizations al-

36. James Clifford, *The Predicament of Culture* (Cambridge, MA: Harvard University Press, 1988), 220.

37. See *Nadja*, 143. See also my "'Not a Nervous Woman': Robert Desnos and Surrealist Literary History," *South Central Review* 20/2 (2003): 111–30.

38. See *André Breton, 42 rue Fontaine* (Paris: CalmelsCohen, 2003).

lowed for flourishes of automatic expression that perhaps speak more loudly than the essays, poems, or objects he produced. It reveals itself to be much more particular in its syntax and vocabulary than his more totalizing gestures of inclusion. Breton's collection mediates his common cause with all those artist outsiders who succeeded in hearing, like him, the subliminal message. With them he shared a "creative paradigm," as Cardinal proposes,[39] an acknowledgment made most fully in December 1965, the year before his death, when he included Wölfli in the list of "seven individuals who inspired the eleventh 'Exposition internationale du surréalisme' at the Oeil Galerie d'Art in Paris."[40]

Through his collection, probably his least consciously mediated work, Breton shared with the artist outsiders whose art he championed and collected what he admired most about them: honest nonverbal communication, an ultimate paradox for such a verbal, even pedagogical man. It was through this nonverbal work of accumulated things, according to the sort of "astonishing dialectical effect" he attributes to the freely expressed work of the confined insane, that Breton left a narrative of the self felt from within, a narrative not in text, but in objects. For a collection also represents; like a language, it tells a story.[41] These things witnessed him, just as he identified them in their authenticity; the relation was intersubjective. Breton evidently believed what Benjamin wrote about the relation between the collector and his objects: "Not that they come alive in him; it is he who lives in them" (67). What Breton, the surrealists, and outsider artists shared most was that *receptivity* he praises so highly, to all forces within or without capable of leading to insight. Beyond Breton's position as a cultural insider, where they differed was in the fact that Breton worked so hard all his life to interpret, as his own analyst one could say, what all those forces were telling him. Through the enhancement of their positioning in his study, now visible in a partial reconstitution in the "Wall of André Breton" display at the Centre Georges Pompidou in Paris, his collected objects resemble the sorts of intensely personal assemblages of everyday things created by artist outsiders—and this partly because the same primitivist aesthetic shaped them.

39. *Parallel Visions* (100). See also Cardinal, "Du modèle intérieur au nid d'oiseau: Breton, Crépin et l'art des médiums," *Art spirite, médiumnique et visionnaire: messages d'outre monde* (Paris: Hoëbeke, 1999), 67–77.

40. Daniel Baumann, "Calculation of Interest," *The Art of Adolf Wölfli* (New York: American Folk Art Museum, 2003), 33.

41. See Mieke Bal, "Telling Objects," *Cultures of Collecting*, 97–115.

It is in this imaginative assortment of high and low works—objects like the boxes made by the mentally ill, stones gathered from the riverbed at Saint-Cirq-Lapopie, and North American kachina dolls, juxtaposed with sculpture by Alberto Giacometti and Man Ray, a mediumistic drawing by Victor Hugo (reproduced in "The Automatic Message"), and paintings by Henri Rousseau, Francis Picabia, Wölfli and Corbaz—that Breton left his most personal statement about outsider art, a statement that the now firm establishment of outsider art as a category allows us to see more clearly.[42] Like artist outsiders Breton surrounded himself with things that spoke to him of himself, that were, for him, "as essential as dreams," to go back to Baudrillard. His persistent idealism matches in some way the innocence he saw in them. His collection now speaks to the public much the way the mediumistic outsider art from "The Automatic Message" does: with the universal language of the most private and personal interior revelation.[43]

42.  Recent books, the journal *Raw Vision*, the annual Outsider Art show in New York City, and the acquisition of outsider art by major museums like the Museum of American Folk Art point to its firm if paradoxical establishment within culture.

43.  Thanks to Roger Cardinal, and also to Jonathan Eburne for conversations about an early draft of this essay, as well as Aube Elléouët and Elisa Breton for allowing me to visit Breton's study in 1992.

# Contributors

MARTINE ANTLE is Professor of French at The University of North Carolina Chapel Hill. She is the author of *Théâtre et poésie surréaliste* (Summa, 1988) and *Les cultures du surréalisme* (Acoria, 2001). She is currently working on a manuscript on women artists of European and Arabic descent.

GEORGIANA M. M. COLVILE is Professor of English at the University of Tours, France and former Professor of French, Film, and Comparative Literature at the University of Colorado, Boulder. She now specializes in the contribution of women to the surrealist movement and has recently published the anthology *Scandaleusement d'elles* (Place, 1999), and editions of Valentine Penrose's writings (Losfeld, 2001), and Simone Breton's writings (Losfeld, 2005). She regularly publishes on film.

KATHARINE CONLEY is Professor of French at Dartmouth College. She is the author of *Automatic Woman: The Representation of Woman in Surrealism* (Nebraska, 1996) and *Robert Desnos, Surrealism, and the Marvelous in Everyday Life* (Nebraska, 2003). She is currently working on a manuscript on ghostliness in surrealism.

JONATHAN P. EBURNE is Assistant Professor of Comparative Literature and English at The Pennsylvania State University, and a 2004–2005 Postdoctoral Fellow at the Center for Humanistic Inquiry, Emory University. He is the author of numerous essays on surrealism and the avant garde, as well as essays on Chester Himes, Raymond Chandler, and William Burroughs. He is currently completing a book entitled "Surrealism and the Art of Crime."

ROBERT HARVEY is Professor of French and Comparative Literature at The State University of New York at Stony Brook. He is also Di-

**YFS 109,** *Surrealism and Its Others,* ed. Katharine Conley and Pierre Taminiaux, © 2006 by Yale University.

recteur de Programme at the Collège International de Philosophie in Paris and the author of *Témoins d'artifice* (L'Harmattan, 2003).

ADAM JOLLES is Assistant Professor in the Department of Art History at Florida State University. He has published several articles on surrealism and exhibition design, and is currently preparing two book manuscripts, one tentatively entitled "Curating Surrealism: The French Avant-Garde in Exhibition" and another collaborative work on the totalitarian museum in prewar Soviet Russia and Nazi Germany.

RAPHAËLLE MOINE is Professor at the Université Paris-X Nanterre in the Département des arts du spectacle. She is the author of *Les genres du cinema* (Nathan, 2002).

RICHARD STAMELMAN is Professor of French and Comparative Literature at Williams College. He is the editor of *The Lure and the Truth of Painting. Selected Essays of Yves Bonnefoy on Art* (Chicago, 1995) and author of *Lost Beyond Telling: Representations of Death and Absence in Modern French Poetry* (Cornell, 1990) and of the forthcoming *The Scented Imagination. The Literature and Culture of Perfume.*

PIERRE TAMINIAUX is an Associate Professor of French at Georgetown University. He is the author of *Robert Pinget* (Le seuil, 1994) and *Surmodernités: entre rêve et technique* (Harmattan, 2003) and is currently at work on a book on the relationship between 20th century French literature and photography.

The following issues are available through **Yale University Press,** Customer Service Department, P.O. Box 209040, New Haven, CT 06520-9040. Tel. 1-800-405-1619. yalebooks.com

69 The Lesson of Paul de Man (1985) $22.00
73 Everyday Life (1987) $22.00
75 The Politics of Tradition: Placing Women in French Literature (1988) $22.00
Special Issue: After the Age of Suspicion: The French Novel Today (1989) $22.00
76 Autour de Racine: Studies in Intertextuality (1989) $22.00
77 Reading the Archive: On Texts and Institutions (1990) $22.00
78 On Bataille (1990) $22.00
79 Literature and the Ethical Question (1991) $22.00
Special Issue: Contexts: Style and Value in Medieval Art and Literature (1991) $22.00
80 Baroque Topographies: Literature/History/ Philosophy (1992) $22.00
81 On Leiris (1992) $22.00
82 Post/Colonial Conditions Vol. 1 (1993) $22.00
83 Post/Colonial Conditions Vol. 2 (1993) $22.00
84 Boundaries: Writing and Drawing (1993) $22.00

85 Discourses of Jewish Identity in 20th-Century France (1994) $22.00
86 Corps Mystique, Corps Sacré (1994) $22.00
87 Another Look, Another Woman (1995) $22.00
88 Depositions: Althusser, Balibar, Macherey (1995) $22.00
89 Drafts (1996) $22.00
90 Same Sex / Different Text? Gay and Lesbian Writing in French (1996) $22.00
91 Genet: In the Language of the Enemy (1997) $22.00
92 Exploring the Conversible World (1997) $22.00
93 The Place of Maurice Blanchot (1998) $22.00
94 Libertinage and Modernity (1999) $22.00
95 Rereading Allegory: Essays in Memory of Daniel Poirion (1999) $22.00
96 50 Years of *Yale French Studies*, Part I: 1948-1979 (1999) $22.00
97 50 Years of *Yale French Studies,* Part 2: 1980-1998 (2000) $22.00

98 The French Fifties (2000) $22.00
99 Jean-François Lyotard: Time and Judgment (2001) $22.00
100 FRANCE/USA: The Cultural Wars (2001) $22.00
101 Fragments of Revolution (2002) $22.00
102 Belgian Memories (2002) $22.00
103 French and Francophone: the Challenge of Expanding Horizons (2003) $22.00
104 Encounters with Levinas (2003) $22.00
105 Pereckonings: Reading Georges Perec (2004) $22.00
106 Jean Paulhan's Fiction, Criticism, and Editorial Activity (2004) $22.00
107 The Haiti Issue (2005) $22.00
108 Crime Fictions (2005) $22.00

-------------------------------------------------------------------

**ORDER FORM**     **Yale University Press,** P.O. Box 209040, New Haven, CT 06520-9040
I would like to purchase the following individual issues:

_____

_____

For individual issues, please add postage and handling:
Single issue, United States $2.75          Each additional issue $.50
Single issue, foreign countries $5.00          Each additional issue $1.00
Connecticut residents please add sales tax of 6%.

Payment of $_____ is enclosed (including sales tax if applicable).


MasterCard no. _____ Expiration date _____

VISA no. _____ Expiration date _____

Signature _____

SHIP TO _____

_____

_____

-------------------------------------------------------------------

See the next page for ordering other back issues. Yale French Studies is also available through Xerox University Microfilms, 300 North Zeeb Road, Ann Arbor, MI 48106.

The following issues are still available through the **Yale French Studies Office,** P.O. Box 208251, New Haven, CT 06520-8251.

19/20 Contemporary Art $3.50

33 Shakespeare $3.50

35 Sade $3.50

39 Literature and Revolution $3.50

42 Zola $5.00

43 The Child's Part $5.00

45 Language as Action $5.00

46 From Stage to Street $3.50

52 Graphesis $5.00

54 Mallarmé $5.00

61 Toward a Theory of Description $6.00

### Add for postage & handling

Single issue, United States $3.85 (Priority Mail)      Each additional issue $1.25
Single issue, United States $1.90 (Third Class)      Each additional issue $ .50
Single issue, foreign countries $3.75 (Book Rate)      Each additional issue $3.00

**YALE FRENCH STUDIES,** P.O. Box 208251, New Haven, Connecticut 06520-8251
A check made payable to YFS is enclosed. Please send me the following issue(s):

Issue no.                          Title                                                      Price

_____

_____

Postage & handling _____

Total _____

Name _____

Number/Street _____

City _____ State _____ Zip _____

- - - - - - - - - - - - - - - - - - - - - - - - - - - - - - - - - - - - - - - - - - - - - - - - - - - - - - - - -

The following issues are now available through Periodicals Service Company, 11 Main Street, Germantown, N.Y. 12526, Phone: (518) 537-4700. Fax: (518) 537-5899.

1 Critical Bibliography of Existentialism
2 Modern Poets
3 Criticism & Creation
4 Literature & Ideas
5 The Modern Theatre
6 France and World Literature
7 André Gide
8 What's Novel in the Novel
9 Symbolism
10 French-American Literature Relationships
11 Eros, Variations...
12 God & the Writer
13 Romanticism Revisited
14 Motley: Today's French Theater
15 Social & Political France
16 Foray through Existentialism
17 The Art of the Cinema
18 Passion & the Intellect, or Malraux

19/20 Contemporary Art
21 Poetry Since the Liberation
22 French Education
23 Humor
24 Midnight Novelists
25 Albert Camus
26 The Myth of Napoleon
27 Women Writers
28 Rousseau
29 The New Dramatists
30 Sartre
31 Surrealism
32 Paris in Literature
33 Shakespeare in France
34 Proust
48 French Freud
51 Approaches to Medieval Romance

36/37 Structuralism has been reprinted by Doubleday as an Anchor Book.
55/56 Literature and Psychoanalysis has been reprinted by Johns Hopkins University Press, and can be ordered through Customer Service, Johns Hopkins University Press, Baltimore, MD 21218.